THE LIBERAL SPIRIT

The Liberal Spirit

Essays on Problems of Freedom in the Modern World

HORACE M. KALLEN

THE NEW SCHOOL FOR SOCIAL RESEARCH

*

A PUBLICATION OF

The New School for Social Research

CORNELL UNIVERSITY PRESS

ITHACA AND NEW YORK * 1948

Preface

ALTHOUGH the papers which compose this book have been produced for different occasions at different times, their theme is the same. They embody some present findings of a single, continuing inquiry into the nature and ground of human freedom and the problems of its survival and growth in the modern world. The inquiry is as old as philosophy. The problems are endemic to all the civilizations of man and chronic to all history. Every so often a turn of events, in this or that part of the world, renders them acute, and liberty becomes a forced and momentous option for men of affairs and politicians as well as for scientists and philosophers. The First World War was such a turn in our own time. The peace which purported to end it took the form of consequences in the leadership, in the political economy, in the cultures, in the religions, and in the school systems of states, in their theory and practice of government and in their foreign relations, which came to a first climax in the Second World War. A new climax is now being mounted. When it may be reached, or that it shall never come, is an issue in part of change and chance, in part of the wisdom and will of those who hold the power among mankind. Meanwhile the men and women who look to them for enlightened courage pass their days in fear among illusions bred by fear and nourished by alarums and excursions of the illusion-makers. They sense of themselves that the ways of their free society are in jeopardy at home, and that its danger is the consequence of a totalitarian menace abroad; but they do not

v

of themselves see, nor have they been convincingly shown, how the continuing crisis of freedom may be overcome by faith acting without illusion.

I myself became aware of the depth and import of the crisis when I traveled in Italy and Russia and Poland and Palestine during 1926 and 1927. I had a chance then to look at the lives and labors of the peoples under the directives of the new orders shaped to the new doctrines and disciplines. And I had the occasion to talk with Mussolini and Gentile, and with divers Russian scholars and functionaries. I set down these experiences and my reactions to them in my *Frontiers of Hope,* a book that fell stillborn from the press. I became preoccupied with the crisis of freedom for the transatlantic world and its meaning for the national being here. Whatever I might be studying or thinking about, the problem kept intruding itself. Looking back, I feel with surprise that I seem to have dealt with hardly anything else.

The essays and addresses composing this book are a part of my dealings over the years. They were done for college classes, learned societies, university celebrations, meetings of personnel managers, and the like. One was prepared for the centenary of the Cooperative Movement; another for that of the University of Buffalo. Some concern themselves with the liberal spirit, and with the freedom which is central to it, as essential experiences. Others deal with interaction between them and institutions such as the state, the church, industry, science, art. Others discuss the interplay of all of them and its consequences to freedom as fact and as ideal. Some have never been printed before. Others have appeared in this or that journal or this or that collective book.

My special thanks go to Professor Milton R. Konvitz of the New York State School of Industrial and Labor Relations at Cornell University, without whose interest the papers would never have been assembled nor this book prepared.

H.M.K.

26 April 1948

The kindness of the following publishers in granting permission to quote from their publications as listed is appreciated: This is the Army, Inc., "My British Buddy" by Irving Berlin; Haldemann-Julius Publications, "The Warfare of Religion against Science" by H. M. Kallen; University of Buffalo, "Modernity and Liberty" by Kallen; *The New Leader*, "The Liberal Spirit" by Kallen; *Gazette des Beaux Arts*, "Freedom and the Artist" by Kallen; Institute for Religious and Social Studies, "Of Humanistic Sources of Democracy" by Kallen, from *Foundations of Democracy*.

Contents

THE LIBERAL SPIRIT

The Liberal Spirit

THE WORD "liberal" is in active circulation again! We are admonished about "liberal" education. We are exhorted about a "liberal" political program. We are warned against the "liberal illusion." We are invited to share the bounties of "the liberal spirit." What with the apostles of the pedagogy of St. John's College in Maryland, the prophets of the Liberal party, the fraters of the Church Militant, and the philosophic renovators of the "liberal tradition," the liberal spirit, or liberalism, is proclaimed at one and the same time to be the cause of all evil and the bringer of every good.

To one writer this liberal spirit is an attitude toward life which has a history of 2,500 years; an attitude

which emphasizes the primary importance of the person, the freedom of the individual, free press, free speech, constitutional government, tolerance, the scientific spirit of inquiry, the rational outlook, social reform, popular education, a relativistic philosophy, and ethico-social religion.[1]

It is an attitude exemplified by personages as diverse as Origen and Voltaire, Erasmus and Dewey, Paine and Darwin. It underlies progress and modern civilization. It is the spirit wherein Jefferson's Jesus and Shelley's Prometheus are one, the spirit which sets men free and makes them friends.

Other oracles, such as the president of the University of Chicago and his companions in the faith, see these compo-

---

[1] Fred G. Bratton, *The Legacy of the Liberal Spirit*.

nents of the liberal spirit as materialism, not morality; causes of decadence, not progress; war, not peace; license, not liberty. They insist that if men are to be free and at peace, they must be indoctrinated in a universal and eternal doctrine, expressed in a timeless literature, according to an unchanging authoritarian discipline.

Perhaps they are finding aid and comfort for this dogma of theirs in George Santayana's recent publication, *Persons and Places*. This bitter and beautiful book is the judgment which a philosopher passed from the remoteness of his eighty-first year upon the powers of place and persons that he believed made him what he is today. His recollections convey little love, much frustration, defeat, and flight. They do not consummate the author's mature vision and his optimal work; rather do they distort and deny those. The beloved teacher I remember is very little the figure he shapes in this book. The true consummation of his inner and outer ways is to be found rather in the disguise of them which he has called *The Last Puritan*. George Santayana was the last Puritan, and that novel is, morally, a truer autobiography than the bitter book which he presents as autobiography. For in a sense, the novel was an utterance of the liberal spirit; the autobiography is an aversion from it. Reflecting upon his father's anticlericalism, the recluse of the Convent of the English Blue Nuns declares:

Liberalism, Protestantism, Judaism, positivism all have the same ultimate aim and standard. It is prosperity, or as the Lutherans put it, union with God at our level, not at God's level. The thing all these schools detest is the ideal union with God at God's level, proper to asceticism, mysticism, Platonism, and pure intelligence which insists on seeing things under the form of truth and of eternity.

But pure intelligence, Platonism, mysticism, asceticism, are not names for ideas or events; they are names for human attitudes toward ideas and events. They are ways of taking ideas and events, and anything in experience may be taken in those ways. Thus Santayana himself takes Matter mystically, ascetically, Platonically, in terms of pure intelligence. Orthodox Christians so take the Trinity; Judaists the Torah; Hegelians the State; Marxists the Dialectic of Matter; Nazis the Nazi Race as against the human race; Catholics the Pope and the Roman Catholic Church. Hence, when it comes to identifying "God's level" or "the form of truth and eternity," this regularly turns out to be some particular establishment, doctrine, and discipline of some particular society of men who demand that also all other men should treat their idol ascetically, mystically, Platonically and in terms of pure intelligence.

Now the spirit of man becomes liberal when it recognizes this psychological and historic fact. Then the important thing ceases to be the idea or event so taken. The important thing becomes the mind's freedom to choose which to take from any and all ideas and events. When Protestantism made the right of private judgment its fighting faith, it was this freedom and not property that it took ascetically, mystically, etc. When liberalism enlarged the field of private judgment, free inquiry and experiment to embrace all other thoughts and things as well as those of religion, it was this freedom which it made its fighting faith.

This freedom defines for the liberal spirit both its goal and it ways of reaching its goal. For that spirit, prosperity can signify only as it facilitates or obstructs this freedom; the doctrines and disciplines of churches, the theories and techniques of governments, the professions and practices of business enterprises are all to be rejected or changed, insofar as they facilitate or obstruct this freedom. For the liberal spirit, "God's level" is the level of this freedom. Alone upon it and only through it are "the form of truth and of eternity" to be attained. Upon it no particular idea or event no person, church, or race, or state, or class can be more divinely chosen or divinely gifted than any other. Each, an individuality different from the others, is the equal of the others in status and liberty. None is entitled to greater privilege or endowed with greater authority than any other. To the liberal spirit the existence of such privilege and authority or the pretension to them is a fall from "God's level" and a menace to freedom.

Naturally, the liberal spirit must be anathema where such pretensions obtain, and where such privilege and authority exist. In those places, liberty can consist only in assent, not in free inquiry; in belief, not in reason; in repetition, not in variation; in conformity, not in spontaneity; in obedience, not in initiative. In those places—be they Nazidom, Spain, Portugal, the Argentine, Russia, Vatican City, Yemen, Quebec, or Japan—variation, free inquiry, reason, spontaneity, and initiative are denounced as license. They constitute what Louis Veuillot called "the liberal illusion" and are exorcised by this or that Monsignor as "satanic and antisocial error." In those places it is the depth of Satanism to disregard requirements of institutions based on claims of authority from God on the ground of loyalty to merely human institutions. Some of the disciples of Louis Veuillot held that only "When the Pope thinks, it is God who meditates in him." But this might be said of the Führer of any authoritarian cult. Leo XIII's demand [2] is representative here of all such authoritarian power in all times. It was a demand for "complete submission and obedience of will to the Church and to the Roman Pontiff as to God himself." A civilization failing to render such submission could be only worthless and meaningless. Nevertheless there is not a single sect or party that denounces free society and the liberal

---

[2] *Great Encyclical Letters of Leo XIII,* pp. 185–193.

4

spirit as evil and corrupt that does not feed and grow fat upon this evil and corruption. Louis Veuillot had admonished the liberals of his day: "Upon your principles you are bound to tolerate us; upon ours we are right to persecute you." He intended to put them between the horns of a dilemma: to be true to the principle of freedom and thus make the way sure for the defeat of the principle by its enemies; or to oppose and suppress the enemies of freedom and thus themselves defeat their own principle for liberals. Much of the disrepute into which the liberal spirit has fallen and many of the charges of inconsistency, weakness, defeatism, cowardice which have been leveled at its spokesmen are due to their acquiescence in this grotesque sophistry; and are due to their failure to recognize that there is nothing in the principle of freedom that requires its own extinction.

John Stuart Mill had exposed that fallacy in his *Essay on Liberty*, when he inquired whether a human being might freely choose to become a slave; and decided that such a choice, being an abdication of liberty (which is the constant and growing power of free choice), was ruled out as nullifying precisely that which free choice affirms.

But Mill's argument was incidental to other issues and its intent was not heeded. Freedom as a goal came to be taken for granted. The interest of liberals concentrated upon ways and means of maintaining and enlarging the state of freedom. Since there is a dynamic connection between the liberties of men and the conditions of their lives and labor, liberal attention concentrated on social and political reforms of those conditions, and liberal theory and practice often undertook and justified institutional concentrations of responsibility and authority, which the liberal spirit had begun by challenging.

The current name for this interest is *security*. Its character

5

is far less a matter of the objective national economy than of the subjective personal psychology. In many areas of endeavor, since the turn of the century and especially between the two world wars, this concern over security became pathological; men of liberal disposition came to believe that it was more democratic to be safe than free, that freedom was the means and safety the end.

Of course, this was manna from heaven for the diverse enemies of the liberal spirit, and they fed well on it. Their tradition, their historic attitudes and present disposition and practices came to have a curious validity in the thinking of even the most liberal of minds. There was, for example, the late Justice Oliver Wendell Holmes. A paragraph from his famous dissent in the Schenck Case is quoted practically every time freedom of speech is discussed. But the quotation invariably begins in the middle of the paragraph, with the phrase, "But when men have realized that time has upset many fighting faiths . . ." In the perspective of the sentences which precede this one, its meaning is not quite that which the quoters intend. Let me set down here those ignored sentences:

Persecution for the expression of opinion seems to me perfectly logical. If you have no doubt of your premises or your power and want a certain result with all your heart, you naturally express your wishes in law and sweep away all opposition. To allow opposition by speech seems to indicate that you think the speech impotent, as when a man says he has squared the circle, or that you do not care wholeheartedly for the result, or that you doubt either your power or your premises.

I do not know of any other instance in which this liberal of liberals, far beyond the most earnest and laborious of his brethren, living or dead, on the High Court of the nation, has attained such a perfection of error regarding the rela-

6

tionships of complete certainty and absolute power to their environment of thoughts and things. If Mr. Holmes is right, then freedom has been at all times and in all places founded on weakness, the liberal spirit has been the spirit of impotence, and logic, loyalty, and piety are qualities of the infallibilist, the dogmatist, and the inquisitor alone. But he is not right. Far from being perfectly logical, persecution for the expression of opinion is, in the infallible, utterly illogical. If you are sure you have the truth, if you are certain of it beyond every peradventure of a doubt, then you know you need do nothing yourself to cause your truth to prevail.

The more devoted you are to the result, the more certain you are about your power and premises, the more calmly and serenely you rest in this devotion and security, the more completely you are on "God's level," seeing things under "the form of truth and of eternity." The others—the different, the opposition—are powerless to make any difference to your faith and ways. You go about your business so confident, so serene, so secure in your own truth that you are tolerant and heedless of the others' errors. The sure sign of your certainty is that opposition to it cannot and does not trouble you. Living, you let live and help live. This has been the way of the true believers, the true mystics in all times and all places.

But if you know in your heart that your infallibility is only a pretension and not a fact; that your truth cannot stand on its own merits, nor by its own powers prevail over its competitors and alternatives; if, in fact, you do not care wholeheartedly for the result and doubt both your powers and your premises, then you do not trust your truth and you fear its opponents and alternatives. Then you persecute the different. Then you undertake to suppress and to destroy the different. In order to strengthen it and make it prevail, you

7

add to whatever inward merit your doubtful faith may have all the force and fraud you can muster. This has been the way, throughout history, of priests and kings claiming specific authority from God.

Now doubt is also the inner condition of the liberal spirit. It acknowledges every doctrine and discipline, and it denies the claim to special privilege of any. But it does not cover up its sense of the equal reality of alternatives by a fear-born aggression on behalf of one, nor does it claim in the name of that one the right to persecute, enslave, and destroy the others. What it believes in beyond any doubt is the equal right of all to equal opportunity to make good their claims on their *own* power, by their *inward* merit. Thus, Communism is neither disproved by constant aggression against Communists outside of Russia, nor proved by the persecution of non-Communists inside of Russia. Nazism is not proved by the sadistocratic handling of non-Nazis by Nazis: only the nature of the Nazis is proved. Persecution, wherever it occurs, establishes only the power and cunning of the persecutor, not the truth and worth of his belief. Those develop only in freedom and through freedom.

It is an uncompromising devotion to the idea of equal liberty as both the means and the end of life that characterizes the liberal spirit. Whatever opposes this equal liberty, the liberal spirit must necessarily oppose. Its labor is always to keep the ways of life and thought open and free. To maintain this openness, this freedom, is the liberal spirit's fighting faith, and of all the faiths men set their hopes upon, this is the only one that time does not upset but confirms.

Modernity and Liberty

E VERY so often, when I come upon the word *problem* in a work of philosophy or social science, I experience wonder. The works, as a rule, evince no more genuine curiosity than a catechism nor are more given to doubt than a multiplication table. Their problems seem to follow from their solutions, not their solutions from their problems. The answers are all known in advance, so that the questions they settle seem to be rhetorical and the reasoning which leads to them but the dialectics of a foregone conclusion. Their argument moves in a circle, the self-confirmation of dogmatic certainty. Yet they repeat the word *problem* as automatically and as frequently as the personal pronoun, with the consequence that the natural or common meaning of the word is stood on its head, and *problem* designates the formal or systematic elaboration of the unproblematical. Seeking the causes of this paradox, I can find no more satisfactory explanation than our spontaneous aversion to the problematical. Innately we prefer belief to doubt and certainty to uncertainty; we feel safer with ordered sequence than with indeterminate change; repetitive necessary connection gives us assurance; innovative spontaneous variation does not.

When the Greeks first used the word, they meant by *problem* some thing or event thrown unexpectedly into experience, breaking up its coherencies, arresting its flow, interposing alternatives, and creating difficulties. They

9

meant an occurrence bringing the smooth, sure action of the personality to deliberation and questioning, calling it to the task of finding new and different ways of going and getting on in a world which the event's coming has altered and thus disordered. And in the daily life of men ever since, *problem* has named just this quality of experience. Insofar, in fact, as freedom signifies a break in the continuity of a sequence, differences in its quality or direction, an intrusion of conflict into order or of harmony into disorder, the irruption of the obscure or unknown into the clear and known, the happening of problems points to the reality and power of freedom. The struggle for solutions suggests a battle *for* freedom *from* freedom, an effort to overrule one freedom by another. Without freedom, no alternatives and no problems, and no solutions.

For if the solution of problems is not a self-liberation from another by means of the control and regulation of that other's freedom, what is it? Solutions must repristinate the smoothness, the ease, the continuity of the flow of experience. They take many forms. In the Great Tradition they embody action which brings conflict to harmony, disorder to order, contingency to necessity, diversity to unity. They undertake to make such determinations of the indeterminate and such fixations of the flowing, as to bring the incomplete and unbounded to completion and finality. They seek to bind the fluid singularities of events and experience into postulated universal systems of eternal law. Each such system is, however, itself a singular event and soon or late it is confronted by one or more rivals claiming to do the same job better. Their tradition, nevertheless, tells, for each, of believers whose unshaken faith trusts in it, though it slay them.

Other solutions are more moderate, more sober. Though they serve the same needs as those of the Great Tradition,

10

their proponents give up all pretense at universality, eternity, and finality. Solutions of this type, consequently, do not look to any liquidation of the problematical. They work rather on the basis of an acquiescence in their own contingency: they recognize that each unification of the diverse into the general and of the singular into the universal is itself a concrete and singular event subject to the challenge of alternatives; subject, hence, to treatment which, if successful, would for the time being at least orchestrate it with its challengers. Often they acknowledge the unique, the irreconcilable, the indeterminable, and sometimes they achieve their intention by discussing and liberating the Many rather than assimilating them into a One. Solutions of this kind we usually call scientific, and the way to them we call the method of science.

*   *   *

Now science is first and last the birthmark of modernity, its unique fingerprint and differentia. The world in which we live and move and have our being may be One World. But it is not one modern world. Modernity is a quality and form of human living far more surely than it is a date in history. To identify the modern as merely of the present time is to confuse the modern with the contemporaneous. But most of what is contemporary is not modern; a little, a very little, of what is modern can be discerned in the remote past of the historian. The qualities of existing men, the ways and works of existing societies, their manners and customs, their mores and religions and arts and sciences, their total cultures, though they exist *now*, at today's front of onmoving time, came to their characteristic forms of being and doing at different moments in man's trajectory. Though they are all contemporary, and all on the same plane of present existence, some remain as eolithic as a

11

cockroach, others as neolithic as a mastodon, others continue relatively unaltered from the age of bronze and the age of iron, from Hellenistic times or the times of imperial Rome. Multitudes in the western world remain hardly less medieval than their forebears who lived when Dante wrote his *Comedy* or Aquinas his *Summas;* minorities retain the ways and thoughts that Adam Smith exalted and David Ricardo rationalized. In every area of the globe where men dwell, these societies of different ages with their different ways of life and thought live together as contemporaries, often struggling to shut each other out and cut each other off, sometimes freely exchanging the thoughts and things of their ways of being, always, willy-nilly, responding to each other now with hindrances and again with help. Wherever you turn—to Australia, to South Africa, to India or China or Russia or France or Great Britain or Scandinavia or Germany or the United States—you will find this contemporaneity of successive and different cultural moments of history and prehistory; savagery and barbarism and antiquity and medievalism and modernity side by side in varying groups of various sizes, some inert and only just surviving like the pith and inward rings of a tree; others with the forward thrust of growth in them, like the tree's outermost living edge. The modern world *is* modern, not because it has the quality of modernity through and through, but because whatever power not of survival merely but of change and growth it may possess has its authentic seat in modernity. The moderns are a minority among their contemporaries. They are, however, the potent, pace-setting minority, the forerunners and shapers of the future majority. They are the pioneers with whom the rest of the world endeavors to catch up.

This minority defines itself not only by its faith in the forms and findings of science, but also by its commitment to three other rules of human association which follow from the scientific outlook and scientific method. The first of these is democracy. The second is industrialism. The third is peace. Science, democracy, industrialism, and peace together constitute the differentiae of the modern mind.

I stress the word *together*. Separately, one or another may be taken into an older organization of doctrine and discipline and there bound to a servile role. In the configurations of such a vassalage, however, it perforce loses its essential character to the whole which has taken it in.[1] Though it retain the outer shape, it has lost the vital principle of its being. One need only think of how the words *science, democracy,* and *peace* were employed by the German Nazis and the Spanish Falangists; which meanings fall away, and which replace them among the Soviets, in Vatican City, or in the Kuomintang.

This vital principle is openness, mobility in all the relationships of men and ideas. To the unmodern mind, the real world is a closed hierarchical order ever one and the same, self-containing and self-contained. To the unmodern mind change is an illusion of our insufficiency and the flow of time but secondary, derivative and misleading; at best but "the moving image of eternity." To the unmodern mind nature is an artifact as artificial as one of Picasso's landscapes; nature is a mutable product of an immutable super-

---

[1] For example, science in the Roman Catholic establishment. Conrad Moehlman points out that the Jesuit periodical, *America*, laments the Catholic lack of scientists and scholars proportional to the church's number. *Who's Who* for 1939, he states, lists 748 Unitarians out of 100,000; but only 1,155 Catholics out of 30,000,000. Of 215 Nobel Prizes awarded by 1944, 30 went to Americans; only 3 to American Catholics. Of 1,300 Americans listed in the 7th edition of *American Men of Science*, only 21 are Catholics, and only 11 born in the United States. "The tenets of the church," it is explained, "are not consonant with scientific endeavor."

13

natural. To the unmodern mind the sequences in which this nature moves, the mechanisms which the sciences of nature and man discern, define, and employ are inferior and menial procedures serving eternal purposes whose perfections are the goals at which all process comes to its dead end. The unmodern mind exalts teleology over mechanism and subordinates techniques to agency. It thinks of experience statically, in terms of completion, not dynamically in terms of progression. It refers the weakness and corruption of human nature to the freedom of the human will; it denies that this free will can by its own intent and labor contribute anything to supply its insufficiency. All that at best it can attain is cheerful submission to the inalterable providence which shapes our ends and whose earthly surrogates are church, state, corporation, or other incarnation of rule and power. To fail in this submission is to deserve destruction and death.

The modern mind, on the other hand, thinks of the world as a place without walls, infinite, open, ever-beyond; as boundless and growing, a process ever exceeding itself; that is, the modern mind postulates the endless extensibility of space, the primacy, the reality of time as we feel and experience time. To the modern mind, nature is literally *natura*—original birth and becoming, the succession of events in their spontaneities and configurations. To the modern mind the supernatural is the artifact, a product and derivative of natural processes which science analyzes and accounts for. To the modern mind, the natural and the supernatural alike are stuffs and arrangements of stuffs brought to light as scientific methods imagine, seek out, delineate, test, and verify them. They are experiences given, which compose the ever-altering body of scientific knowledge about nature and man. To the modern mind the modes in which these stuffs join together and the patterns of their

14

association are mechanisms; [2] their compoundings, disso-
ciation, and reunions go on boundless, cumulative, emerg-
ing in new stuffs and orders as they go. In their sequence
no event is of itself higher or lower than any other, none is
better or worse; each follows one that had come before,
each is followed by one that comes after. Each is different
from the others, and each is equally with the others at
once cause and effect. In contrast to the unmodern mind,
the modern mind envisages no event, no being, which is
only cause or only effect. Each has both passion and action.
If, in the unending sequence of experience, each is a determination, it is also equally a determiner.

*　*　*

With this conception of the dynamics of nature came a
mutation in the idea of human nature. Supernatural Man,
the supreme object of divine solicitude, was replaced by
the natural man with his natural rights whose being and
doing were defined and measured no more and no less
than any other event in nature by "the laws of Nature and
of Nature's God." With this assimilation of man to nature

---

[2] The modern disposition is not to abolish teleology but to restate it as a
form of mechanism—in the main of a circular system in which the end
term as effect serves also as the cause of the initiating term. Both connec-
tionism and Gestalt psychology give a pre-eminent place to such relational
structures. They are very useful in the interpretation of physiological
mechanisms such as homeostasis, and they figure extensively in current
studies of physicists and mathematicians. Anthropologists, particularly
cultural anthropologists, are apt to use them unaware. Logically, they postulate a notion of the relations of whole and part in which the whole is
prior to its parts, and the relations of the parts to one another are internal.
This postulate is by no means generally accepted, although the data
whence it is drawn are acknowledged. For the present, the situation is
ambiguous. Interpretations of the whole-part relations as external can and
do give no less satisfactory explanations of circular or teleological events
than the doctrine of internal relations. Ultimately the preference of the
investigator seems the decisive force.

15

went the equalization of all men within nature. "Life, liberty and the pursuit of happiness" came to be thought as the equal rights of different people; as their "inherent and unalienable rights" whatever might be their birth, faith, sex, station, occupation, or history. Privilege and power were made to stand naked without sanction. If some men subjected others to their will, it was by usurpation, not by right. As events in a nature which determines each individual to be what he is, men are at once different from each other and equal to each other. Their association consequently is also a natural event flowing from what they desire and resting on what they are. The dynamic of social relations is a contractual relationship; the basis of institutions and government is consent and participation; and law, as Blackstone suggests in his *Commentaries,* is the instrument by which the different contracting parties guarantee each other their equal rights, especially their equal liberty.[3]

It is in this wise that the naturalization of man brought the idea of the democratization of society. When mechanism displaced teleology in the effective understanding of causes, equality displaced hierarchy and liberty displaced servility in the consequent redefinition of human relations. Those were no longer regarded as fixed, internal, and unalterable. The individual became mobile with the right and

---

[3] Spinoza seems to have formulated what became the characteristic of this ideal. "The ultimate aim of government is not to rule, nor to restrain by fear, nor to exact obedience, but, contrariwise, to free every man from fear, that he may live in all possible security; in other words, to strengthen his natural right to exist and to work without injury to himself or others. No, the object of government is not to change men from rational beings into beasts or puppets, but to enable them to develop their minds and bodies in security, and to employ their reason unshackled; neither showing hatred, anger, or deceit, nor watched with the eyes of jealousy and injustice. In fact, the true aim of government is liberty" (*The Theologico-Political Tractate*).

the power to pass freely from class to class, occupation to occupation, cult to cult, and country to country. The fact of the servile state began to be reshaped to the ideal of a free society. What we call democracy became first a vision, then a plan, and finally a present event struggling for growth and survival and surely, even if slowly and painfully, achieving them.

For the realization of this plan the machine has figured in critical but ambivalent modes. Its role in the making of the democratic way of life has been at once facilitation and suppression, propulsion and nullification. The industrial revolution and the democratic revolution overlapped in time and interpenetrated in traits. The former, like the latter, was seeded in the displacement of teleology by mechanism. Thinking events dynamically as a progression of cause-effect-cause-effect, men of the seventeenth and eighteenth centuries came to assimilate the perceptions and measures of Galileo and the mathematical laws of Newton with long-ignored observations and prescriptions in the recipe books of carpenters and builders, of painters, mechanics and pilots, of jewelers and smiths and artillerists. It is not for nothing that Newton conceived his universe in the image of a clock, and his God in the likeness of a clockmaker. From the seventeenth-century clockmaker with his tools and skills to the twentieth-century engine or airplane factory with its conveyer system and its tools and skills, the waves of mutation swell from change to change, with an ever-increasing momentum, multiplicity, and variety.

The mechanical works of man, invention after invention, supervene upon each other with unpredictable consequences to the life of man. They have changed him, where they prevail, from an independent farmer or herder or artisan into a dependent member of a factory organization.

17

The division of labor which the machine enables and the factory channels has thinned him down from a man living his life into a machine tender earning his living; it has diminished his vocational need for knowledge and reduced his skill to a few simple repetitive acts. By making of those, items in the clocklike sequence of the conveyer system, it has given him a fixed station in an associative order of enforced co-operation, a co-operation required not by the understanding and decision of the men at work, not even of the managers, but by the structure of the machine and the layout of the factory which the operation of that tool determines. The associations in which this sets a man are imposed, not chosen; they are external to his awareness and kept secret from his understanding. He stands no longer as the master of his tools and materials, as an artisan or craftsman with a proper name. He stands as a factory hand with a number. He is a psychosomatic gadget attached to a gargantuan automatic instrument. He is the servant of his tools and materials. He is exclusively a producer. But though a producer, he is not permitted to know either the components of his product, nor their original nature, nor their sources, nor how they came to him, nor what they cost, nor what it costs to make them over into his product, nor who buys his product, nor at what price. This knowledge is the monopoly of management. It is private property, a patent right, a trade secret, social and economic power. By virtue of it, it is the management and not the men, it is the factory and not the factory hands that is the producer. The hands count, like the cogs of a wheel, merely as interlocking fractions of a wound-up whole. The hands are *labor*, but management is industry. And because this is the case, labor tends to be hired and fired at the will of managements. Having established no rights in their indus-

18

try, laborers have no power over their own support.[4] It is in order to attain this power and to share in the knowledge of the whole, where they otherwise count merely as replaceable parts, that they form the conscious free organizations of workers called trades unions, with which they strive to guide and reshape the human effects of the unconscious hierarchical organization of work called industry.

Factory organization of work has brought city organization of life. Cities multiply and grow. The modern world is so pre-eminently an urban world because it is an industrial world. Men of industrial society live together as they work together, in great multitudes, interdependently, yet emotionally and intellectually isolated and unaware. As the factory is the workplace where the mechanic works by day to earn his living, the great city has become the market place where the mechanic spends by night to live his life. The fruits of his day's labor are consumed in his night's leisure. The industrial worker, automatized in his role of producer, is therein a bondsman. But unlike the pre-industrial slave or serf, he becomes a free man in his role of consumer. Whereas his forebears lived on one, modern man lives on two, for the most part, incommensurable levels. The first is essentially a means; the other is genuinely an end. He is a producer and a consumer and he produces in order to consume. But machinery has set up an unprecedented dichotomy between production and consumption. It has led to the idea of an economy of abundance in thoughts and things, in goods, services, and ideas. Contracting space and condensing time, bringing all the diverse products of all the cultures of the world within the reach of industrial men, machinery has inverted the natural

---

[4] See *The Federalist*, no. 10.

and historic relationships between them. It has exalted production into the end and degraded consumption into the means. Thus it has brought on a sharp conflict between the economy of industry and the nature of man. For we are born consumers, and all our doings, our thinking, playing, eating, drinking, fighting, loving, making things, and destroying things, insofar as they are spontaneous and not compelled, are consummatory. For example, we own an instinct of workmanship, which skill and knowledge channel and express, by whose virtue every craftsman is a creative artist, and every artist a free man consuming his energies in free activities. Since even the serf and slave of preindustrial times owned a modicum of this inner freedom, the values of day-life and of night-life were not separated and opposed for him. But they are so for us. They are so for us because modern production is mass production based on the division of labor. Its morcellation into ever more numerous and separate steps creates a vacuum for the instinct of workmanship; its automatic machines replace craftsmanship by engineering and demote knowledge and skill to superfluities. At the same time they enable men to produce infinitely more. Where an economy of abundance obtains and is left free to work itself out, it does in fact reduce the hours of labor, increase the hours of leisure, and raise the standard of living beyond all precedent. But it simultaneously deepens the distinction between living and earning a living, between leisure and labor, between consumption and production. Consequent on the psychic distance which separates these modes of human activity and ensuing upon their correlative forms of association—i.e., private monopolies, state trusts, and the like—come their business cycles with their booms and busts, their *crises plethoriques,* with the familiar "starvation amid plenty." Supervening upon these come then the plans to resolve

20

them devised by medievalists, communists, and fascists, and implemented with such tragic consequences in lands like Spain and Poland, Russia, Italy, and Germany.

* * *

For these plans, born from a discontent with some of the consequences of science and democracy, involved also the rejection of the fourth attribute of the modern mind—its pacifism. As there have always been lovers of freedom, so there have always been believers in peace, but in peace as a matter of faith, peace, the providence of God, not peace, the work of man. Widespread effort to achieve an effective organization of peace follows the rise of science and runs together with democracy and industry. Regardless of how successful this effort has been, it is signally an attribute of the modern mind.

Scorn of war, disgust with war's motives and causes, plans for the organization of a society of nations under international law began to be conspicuous among the wits and sages of the eighteenth century, of whom Voltaire and Kant are types. Associations to prevent war or to maintain peace were formed soon after the democratic revolutions in the United States and in France. The first peace society of record was organized in New York in 1815, and re-enforced by similar societies in other states. These, after a time, united as the American Peace Society of which Thomas Jefferson became the leading member. By that time peace societies had already been organized in Great Britain, in France, and somewhat later another was organized in Switzerland. In 1843 representatives of these met in London for the first International Peace Congress. From then on peace societies multiplied. The end of our own Civil War, in which abolitionists who were also pacifists played a heroic part, saw such societies springing up everywhere.

21

Peace between nations and democracy within nations were felt to be interdependent. The belief became general that war was an instrument only of despotism and privilege, that it upheld tyranny, that its preparation and conduct destroy the liberties of men. All sorts of voluntary movements seeking these liberties became at the same time opponents of war. In the first Woman's Peace League, formed in London in 1895, opposition was organized on the basis of the interest and disposition of woman as woman. Studies by publicists and others demonstrated the prohibitive costs of war, its unprofitableness, and its other even more nasty traits. Mr. Andrew Carnegie, the iron monger, dedicated a large part of his fortune to the establishment of a Peace Foundation. Mr. Alfred Nobel, the munitions maker, offered income from his for a peace prize. That men waged war, nevertheless, is another story.[5] What is important is that first, volunteers, private persons and groups, and then governments, pushed into action by the pressure of a public sentiment generated and crystallized by these volunteers, struggled, purposefully aware, to prevent war and to organize peace.

The League of Nations was a fruit of these struggles. If the governments which pledged themselves to enforce its covenant and to cherish its organs and spirit broke faith with it, the peoples they governed struggled for an organization of peace and a rejection of war nevertheless. In 1921, citizens of sixty-eight countries formed the War Resisters' International. Others joined leagues to enforce peace, others League of Nations' Associations and Unions. They created a climate of opinion which compelled the pious professions of the Kellogg Pact whereby the high contracting parties "renounced war as an instrument of policy." The most romantically logical among the peace

---

[5] See H. M. Kallen, "Of War and Peace," *Social Research*, Sept. 1939.

lovers and war haters gave this pact a poignant personal
immediacy when, in 1934, they organized the Peace Pledge
Union. The members of this Union swore "we renounce
war and never again, directly or indirectly, will we support
or sanction another," and found before many years had
passed that if they really wanted peace they must fight
for it. Many of them died heroically on the battlefields of
World War II. When Woodrow Wilson declared that
America and the Allies were fighting World War I to "make
the world safe for democracy," he was expressing the deep
conviction of modern men everywhere that war and freedom cannot live together,[6] that peace too is the organization of liberty.

Such, in sum, are the differentiae of modernity—science,
democracy, machine industry, peace. Each has its own individuality, its own irreduceable singularity of procedure
and goal. All, nevertheless, are sprung from a common impulsion and own a common drive.

This impulsion, this drive, is freedom. For science it is
freedom of thought, of inquiry; of expression, experimentation, and communication; take away any of these, and science ceases to be discovery of the new and hardens into
repetition of the old. For democracy it is equal liberty for
different persons, different beliefs, and different associations, in organizing and altering government; in defining,
registering, and implementing fundamental law and public
policy; take away any of these and government of the people, by the people, for the people becomes government by
a sect, a party, a man, a bureaucracy, an economic establishment, for that privileged minority; government by coercion replaces government by consent; exploitation of
Have-nots by Haves replaces government by consent; ex-

---

[6] See H. M. Kallen, *The Future of Peace* (Chicago, 1941); *The Structure of Lasting Peace* (Boston, 1918).

23

ploitation of Have-nots by Haves replaces the general welfare. So also, freedom is the impulsion and drive of machine industry. For the improvement, the diversification, and the extended use of machinery depend in the last resort on the free enterprise of the inventor, the investor, the production engineer, the mechanic, the salesman, and the free choice of the consumer; take away any one of these, and an industry contracts from competitive expansion into monopolistic immobility; quality falls, prices rise; invention stagnates. Without freedom an economic *rigor mortis* sets in. And lastly, freedom is the going and the goal of world peace, since, on the record, peace is democracy among sovereign states, democracy is peace. For an international order, which should establish and keep secure the safety and well-being of the peoples of the different nations, would rest on a union of the nations and on laws agreed to by those nations which pledge and seek to procure for each party to the union that parity of liberty and right which democratic states pledge and seek to secure for each of their individual citizens. Take away any of these and peace becomes a preparation for war.

In sum, the four differentiae of modernity reduce to expression of one—freedom.

*   *   *

What then is this freedom which signalizes the ways of modern man? The word and its synonyms are as ancient as civilization itself. Is the idea, is the experience of which the words are the signs, as old? If the philosophers and theologians may be trusted, they are not. Free men were far less numerous in the slave economies of antiquity than in ours, and they thought of their freedom or liberty rather as doing with a will what their community or their cosmos required them to do, willy-nilly. Their freedom consisted in per-

24

sonal harmony with the corporate discipline into which
they were born and in which they grew up. This harmony
could not be a consequence of choice because there was,
they believed, no real alternative to prefer. Whatever it
was, they had to take it, they could not leave it. Be it their
city, or be it their universe, if they were wise they would
gladly acquiesce in its inescapable order and submit to its
inalterable law; if they were fools, they would resist and
nevertheless do what must be done anyhow. So Socrates
drank the hemlock, and Epictetus wore the shackles of
slavery. Their freedom was glad or sad submission to authority and necessity, but submission. It was definable only with
respect to authority and necessity. Christian liberty was
nothing else.[7] Although the idea of it involved the notion of
free will, to achieve salvation the freedom must be futile
and the will, will-less. For the grace which saves is the send-
ing of a God who is all, sees all, and does all. Man's peace
is in God's will, and his liberty is not a determination in his
own nature but a predestination by divine nature. It is
libertas obedientiae.

There are many who think that this digestion of liberty
in authority or necessity makes nonsense of liberty and
banishes it from the world. But this is not the case. Not the
existence, only the seat of liberty has been denied. It has
been shifted from the individual to his community, from
man to nature or to God. For authority is an attribute of
authorship and authorship is the spontaneous power of
originating, of creating, of maintaining, and hence of giv-
ing shape, direction, movement, and goal to the creature
resulting. When this power is held to be self-containing and
self-contained, it is ineffable. Nothing can justify it, nothing
can account for it, nor does it require explanation or justi-

---

[7] See E. Gilson, *The Spirit of Mediaeval Philosophy* (New York, 1936),
ch. xv.

fication. Its authority is then authentic and absolute, free. Men can only hear and obey. In all human issues, it is the court of last resort. Those issues arise where a secondary authority holds sway whose power is a delegated power, a power derivative, not original; received, not spontaneous, having the authority of an agent, not a principal. Power holders in states, churches, schools, corporations, castes, races, and occupations do sometimes claim authentic originality for their exercise of authority; but for the most part they justify their domination and rule of others and explain their ascendancy and influence by referring them to primal springs in nature or God. Commanding and coercing others, the holders of authority, be it original or derived, are themselves not subject to the laws they ordain. The freedom of the lawgiver is still original freedom, of quite another kind than the freedom of the law taker. The freedom of the lawgiver is the authentic liberty, without which *libertas obedientiae* would be meaningless if not impossible.

To the premodern mind, then, alike the religious and the secular, liberty was prevailingly *libertas obedientiae*. When identified with willing conformation to this or that pattern of social organization, it was freedom by authority for authority. When identified with willing conformation to the rule of the causal order of nature, it was freedom as obedience to natural law. Although the romantic philosophers, chiefly Hegel, undertook to make this identification of freedom with coercion acceptable by claiming freedom for the substance and goal of the universe, they accomplished no more at best than a restating of Spinoza's identification of freedom with necessity in the language of their own peculiar mythology. They simply provided new words for old ways of dissolving personal liberty in social authority or natural determinism. They belong with the premoderns.

For modernity rejects this dissolution *au fond*. Modernity inverts this dissolution. The modern way makes freedom in and for the person the first and last thing; it takes all authority and all law to be secondary and derivative. It demotes them from powers that rule into instruments that serve: it accounts for them not as originals with powers and spontaneities in themselves, but as constructs and consequences, as the modes and channels—that is, the methods and proceedings—of freedom. The modern mind is today disposed to envisage freedom as a simple, positive, identifiable but ineffable occurrence in experience, the point of initiation of every other thing that repeats, that develops, and grows, and ends. Habit, law, order, the mechanisms of nature, and the institutions of human nature are all (to the modern mind) organizations of liberty. Although the reasoned manipulations of science have brought physics to a ground without rationality, although they have made of spontaneous chance and uncertain probability the quicksand foundations of all existence, these findings and makings are consummations of the progressive mastery of nature and self-mastery of man which science and technics, democracy and peace signalize. Each in its own domain is an organization of liberty. Given their first classical expression in the beatitudes of the Declaration of Independence,[8] they receive

---

[8] These consist of the seven propositions which the signers of the Declaration held to be "self-evident truths." They define the democratic conception of the relations that should—not *do*—obtain between individuals and the society which they compose. However one may formulate an ultimate philosophy of these relationships, such a philosophy, to be democratic, would have to retain, to develop, and to justify, somehow, the intention of these propositions, which are herewith set down:

1. that all men are created equal,
2. that they are endowed by their Creator with certain unalienable rights,
3. that among these are life, liberty and the pursuit of happiness,
4. that to secure these rights, governments are instituted among men,

today a new turn via the promulgation of the Four Freedoms. I set them down as Franklin Roosevelt said them, one year to a month before the aggression of a treacherous foe struck us down into our second world war.

In the future days, which we seek to make secure, we look forward to a world founded upon four essential human freedoms.

The first is freedom of speech and expression—everywhere in the world.

The second is freedom of every person to worship God in his own way—everywhere in the world.

The third is freedom from want—which, translated into world-terms, means economic understandings, which will secure to every nation a healthy peace-time life for its inhabitants—everywhere in the world.

The fourth is freedom from fear—which, translated into world terms, means a world-wide reduction of armaments to such a point and in such a thorough fashion that no nation will be in a position to commit an act of physical aggression against any neighbor—anywhere in the world.

This is no vision of a distant millennium. It is a definite basis for a kind of world attainable in our own time and generation.

These six sentences designate the problems and define the tasks of the new organization of freedom which our time calls for. The older organizations have done better than many devotees of freedom will acknowledge. In the nature of things more deeply sensitive of the unexpected evils in their consequences than to the expected satisfactions, the freedom lovers regard the spiritual, the moral, and the material state of the modern world as a tragic predica-

---

5. deriving their just powers from the consent of the governed,

6. that whenever any form of government becomes destructive of these ends, it is the right of the people to alter or abolish it,

7. and institute new government, laying its foundation on such principles and organizing its powers in such form, as to them shall seem most likely to effect their safety and happiness.

ment into which we sink the deeper the more we labor to lift ourselves from it. Modern freedom, they would have us believe, has brought in its train intellectual confusion, economic monopoly, political bureaucracy, and moral and spiritual materialism, and these overrule our spirit of live and let live, our scientific method and democratic team-play, our swift mobility in space and in society, our better health and enhanced well-being, which are of the abundant fruit of modern liberty wherever it has truly taken root.

The problem of our generation is clearly to discern what freedom is and so to reorganize its ways and works as to bring them to dominance beyond all fear of overthrow.

The Organization of Freedom

I. CREATIVE LIBERTY AND LIBERTAS OBEDIENTIAE IN NATURE

AS COMPARED with modern man, unmodern man lives, and premodern man lived, a narrow, brutish, intolerant, and servile life. Even in Newton's day his knowledge was small, his tools were few, his skills as limited as they were excellent, his movements slow in time and confined in space. His weapons were simple and his armies average, but his wars were no less numerous nor his cruelties less abominable and great. He was certain that an all-wise, all-powerful, just, and loving Providence had shaped his ends to its own immutable divine ones but had nevertheless endowed him with free will. In the measure of his impotence, premodern man believed in his free will.

Most modern men have given up this contradiction and taken on its converse. Most modern men do not believe in their free will. They believe in determinism. Having devised tools and methods for discerning, for measuring, and for foretelling how all nature's forms come about, how they come together, how they stay together, how they come apart, how and at what rate they move, what they do and how they do it, modern men have unveiled the mysteries of cause and efficacy and translated them into naked natural law. Doing this thing, they have achieved the knowledge which is power. By applying this new kind of knowledge to the world around, they have been able to contrive ever-mightier and preciser tools by whose means they could observe and measure events ever more clearly and distinctly and could work on the stuffs of nature ever more fruitfully. Wherever this power of theirs reached out, they were able to transmute the wastes of nature into the wealth of man. With the steam engine and the gas engine they breached the bounds of space and shortened the stretches of time. With the kerosene lamp, the gas burner, the electric bulb, the incandescent tube, they irradiated the night with the brightness of day. With the telegraph, the telephone, the radio, the camera, the motion-picture instrument, the television set, radar, they made communication instant between the farthest places of the earth and threw signals to the stars. Their knowledge of the mechanisms of nature gave them power over the land, the water, the air, and the plants and beasts of the earth. It brought them mastery over sickness and strength against death. Length of years came with it, and also unheard-of devices for diminishing the years. For the knowledge which is power to enlarge and to create is also power to dwarf and destroy. Who is not agitated over men's vastly improved weapons of war, beyond imagination deadly to their fellow men!

So then, on some places of the globe, modern man by the might of his knowledge reshaped nature for the satisfactions of human nature. He freed his life from the tethers by which time, space, and the stuffs and articulations of his surroundings held him bound. He *has* achieved the miracle of making a silk purse out of a sow's ear. He has accomplished an economy of abundance in thoughts and things and he has truly though not successfully striven to make his ways the ways of peace. On many more places of the globe modern man has used his power to harness undated nature as a power to bind unmodern and premodern men in unheard-of bonds. Of the economy of abundance he built at

31

home, he made a base, tooled by science and geared for war, to impose dominion and empire abroad. But at home, such enslavements aside, the consequences of modern man's insight into the determinism of nature has been his liberation as man.

What may be said of the impulsions of this freedom, which takes determinism for its instrument? What does it lead to? Where and how may it go?

Our time resounds with the warnings of Cassandras who prophesy that to these questions science can give no answer. All men, they chant, all values, are indifferent to science, for whose detached and impersonal view abundance signifies no more than scarcity, freedom than bondage, the tyrant than the slave. All are events in an indifferent sequence of cause and effect, and in the scientist's task of searching out measurable specific causes for measurable specific effects, a man is worth only as much as a thing. When psychologists, educators, college administrators equally with personnel managers and employment agents endeavor to define the qualities of men by means of machines that test and measure, do they not use the scientific understanding of nature in order to dissolve personal character into mechanical clockworks? Do they not dissolve the human being into the nonhuman event? Science can free men or enslave them, enrich men or impoverish them, but *which* is not itself a decision within the power of science to make.

The decision is not within the power of science because science, we are told, being the embodiment of modern man's insight into nature, takes determinism for its ground and postulates only uniformity, regularity, repetition in all things. The decision is not within the power of science because technics, being modern man's system of the applications of his embodied insight, postulates mechanism as

32

the ground of works, so that engineers and architects are but machinists *in excelsis*. And our modern psychologists and social scientists, are they, it is asked, anything different? Do they not start from these same postulates in their study of man? Do they not seek for their disciplines the same certainty of belief, the same precision of prediction and control which are the envied excellences of the sciences of nature? To merit the praise which the word *science* and its derivatives carry, the study of man must meet the determinist criteria of the study of the stars and the stuffs and articulations of earth. Until psychology and sociology and economics and politics become as physics and chemistry and biology and mechanics and astronomy, they will not merit the eulogium *science*.

But if they become like unto these, must they not also postulate that what the Declaration of Independence has written down about freedom as a self-evident truth is a self-evident error? Then what becomes of the problems of freedom which so vex our time? Are they not in truth abolished? If determinism is true, must not freedom be false, or else, with all the values men set their hearts upon, outside the realm of science altogether? And if they are outside, what good are the methods and results of science in solving the modern man's problem of freedom? Yet scientific determinist as he is, modern man's care for freedom is far more urgent than that of his unmodern forebears. He does believe with a fighting faith, that freedom *is* an inalienable right of every man, and he has bled and died to vindicate this right throughout modern times. Only, uniquely, in modern times, have free men fought not alone for their own liberties but also to set slaves free as in the American Civil War. Daily modern man experiences freedom, seeks freedom, and uses freedom. So far as living his life goes, scientific determinism has been among his best means to freedom. Can science then make no deliverances about freedom's nature and intent?

So formulated, the question reinstates the dilemma of determinism [1] with which William James challenged philosophers half a hundred years ago, and which he himself learned from the revolutionary French libertarian Charles Renouvier, a generation before. In a world all of whose events are automatic and predetermined—the argument runs—the urge and idea of freedom and its conflict with the idea of determinism must also be automatic and predetermined. The foreordained choice between them cannot fail to lead to momentous consequences for the chooser. Whichever he decides upon, he could not have decided otherwise. Yet the choice of one means necessity, repetition, everlastingly recurring cycles of old thoughts and old things moving in old directions upon old ways. It means there can be no contingencies and no disjunctions nor any true alternatives. It means that control must be error and the very choice which affirms it, illusion. It means that freedom is but the synonym for ignorance. Since events must be the necessary repetition of identicals, a passage from ignorance to knowledge is ruled out. Yet in fact such passages do occur, and in both directions. In fact, illusion is changed over into reality and error is confronted and overruled by truth, and vice versa. Such events strict determinism can neither explain nor explain away. It can only establish the believer as a resigned and submissive do-nothing or as a bullying fanatic. His world is inalterably either the best possible or the worst possible, and no thing in it can be otherwise than it is. Or, its compulsions—which he calls his Fate or Destiny and which he can neither confront nor escape—drive him against all men, and he can-

---

[1] See William James, "The Dilemma of Determinism," in *The Will to Believe* (New York, 1896).

not do otherwise than he does. World and man both, if they move at all, move inalterably to an inalterable end.

The choice of freedom, on the other hand, does not abolish determinism. The choice of freedom only limits and checks determinism. It simply adds to repetition and recurrence spontaneity and originality. It accepts our experiences of chance and contingency as experiences of the real. It takes at its face value the experience of new events confluent with old but not compelled by them; new events initiating new turns upon new ways in new directions toward new alternatives of thoughts or things. The choice of freedom grounds the fact that knowledge does replace ignorance, truth, error, and power helplessness. Choosing freedom, a man can stand up. A man can believe at his own risk and fight for his faith on his own power. Determinism, to this believer, is changed by his belief from a totalitarian metaphysic of existence into a method of understanding and managing an untotalizable existence. It becomes a consequence and vindication of freedom. In the daily life we experience existence now as free, now as determined, and again as both and neither. Carried down from the abstractions of the philosopher to the enterprises of the workaday world, in the daily life the sciences become transvalued from an effort to uncover an inert and immutable order into a succession of determinations, with which by trying out theories, experiments, and verifications and again and again revising them we slowly and assiduously shape new truths and transform old ones into new error. When freedom is the choice, science is realized as an open, imaginative, self-correcting adventure in perception, understanding and management—a free enterprise which works its way through a boundless world on hypotheses that aim at unguaranteed consequences, not at foregone conclusions.

*   *   *

The choice of freedom, thus, and the intellectual explication of what thereupon emerges from it in life and thought are but an extension of every man's ordinary experiences to the ultimacies of his own nature and that of the world where it happened and grew. We may now inquire, what, in these experiences, is freedom positively *known as?*

I am afraid that a satisfactory analytical answer to the question is not available. The *quale* of freedom is elemental. It is given to feeling and seems ineffable. It comes, apparently, not as singular, but in two modes. One mode goes with both *libertas obedientiae* and *creative liberty*. The other mode seems to go only with *creative liberty*. Definitions of freedom impress me as being circular, and assuming one or the other of the experiences they would define. Most definitions add, to statement of the experiential *quale*, statements of the occasions and conditions of its being experienced, but do not reduce its nature to something else. For the most part, philosophers, social scientists, politicians, and ecclesiastics who speak of freedom use it not as a substantive but as a relational term. It figures in their discourse sometimes as a one-one relation, but mostly as a one-many, between the self and other beings, whatever their traits. Sometimes the relation is one of acquiescence, submission; of a liquidation of the self in a not-self; again it is one of checking, dominating, repudiating, or liquidating the not-self, of an alone-making of the self; yet again, it is one of confluence and interpenetration without identification—that is, of orchestration—of the self and not-self.

Every definition of liberty, I think:—classical, Christian, and modern; in every field—psychological, religious, social, political, aesthetic, and scientific—will be found to employ one or another of these relationships. Its freedom will be regularly freedom *from*, freedom *of*, freedom *to*, or freedom *for;* but hardly ever simply *freedom.*[2] Limitations of the not-self appear in the definitions more commonly than facilitations of the self. This implies that when resistance is removed, when interference is excluded, and facilitation occurs, the facilitation is self-facilitation; it implies that the personality then goes on its own power in its own way; that, so to speak, it feeds on itself and grows by what it feeds on; that its power, its going, and its goal are one and the same and are, as such, a process of self-diversification in which energies increase without cause and attainments come without strain. If another, a not-self, should contribute to this state, and itself be enriched in turn, the synergy would be an orchestration, a teamplay or union of the different.

Many have been the efforts to give an analytical account of this state of freedom. All seem to me to have come out in paradoxes and contradictions; and perhaps this outcome flows from the *quale* of freedom and does point to a nature irreducible, if not simple, a nature of which "time" is the commonest sample. Discourse, however, goes on the assumption that inconsistency, unreality and error imply each other. Whatever be the case, if liberty is the inborn and inalienable right it is said to be, if it is anything positive at all in anybody's personal experience, it is this paradox-and-contradiction-occasioning *quale*.

The second kind of experience for which liberty or freedom is the enduring expression seems in many ways polar to the feel of spontaneous and fluent self-differentiation inward to the first. It is what we became aware of when we experience freedom of the will. It is the quality of consciousness that ensues when conflicting alternatives present themselves each with an urgency which admits of no conciliation, which refuses all debate and would shut the

2 See "Freedom and the Artist," pp. 135 *et seq.*

other out and cut it off. The competing urgencies may be impulsions, desires, or passions; they may be sensations, or images, or ideas, or habits, or doctrines and disciplines and ways of life; they may be old tools or new inventions; they may be properties or persons. They thrust equally upon the attention, each seeking the exclusion of the other. They exact a choice. Free will is then an outweighing of one by the other through the act of choosing that other. If that preferred one is the weaker, choice of it is an overpowering of the stronger. Whatever the character of the chosen, "we feel," William James writes,[3] "in deciding, as if we ourselves by our own wilful act inclined the beam. . . . The slow dead heave of the will that is felt in these instances makes of them a class altogether different subjectively. . . ." Decision takes place as an increment of energy beyond that which the precisest calculation could account for; as a manifestation of new power in a system closed by definition to all addition and all diminution. James called such decision "a desolate and acrid sort of act, an excursion into a lonesome moral wilderness."

When a thinker, a soldier, an artist, a scientist, an inventor, a manufacturer, a merchant, a religious prophet, or a religious convert wills to believe his own new vision at his own risk and stakes his survival on his faith, he makes such an excursion. To his fellows he is a hero, or he is a nuisance, a madman, an infidel, a revolutionary, an anarchist, meriting excommunication and the stake. To himself he is certain beyond all certainty of his sanity and of his truth and its power to win to a life more abundant in whose achievement he will enjoy that first state of freedom. Though it slay him, he trusts in his vision and will not give it up.

---

[3] See William James, *The Principles of Psychology* (New York, 1904), vol. II, ch. xxvi.

Clearly, it is initiations of this sort which have carried the modern world to life and growth. There has come with them, also, an inversion of the preferences of attitude and method which exalted the sciences of nature over the sciences of man. Time was when both steadily belittled their springs and sought to bring their doing and being ever closer to the universal determinism which was their central postulate. That the social sciences did envy and emulate the sciences of nature; that their protagonists heroically tried to achieve by dialectic and rationalization what the apparently insurmountable difficulties of experimentation, measurement, and verification kept them from trying in their fields, that they did strive to vindicate themselves as scientists through successful prediction and control—this is a matter of record. The record has, however, not yet sufficiently underscored the fact that in due course they turned away from the dialectic and rationalization and invented new methods proper to their subject matter, methods growing out of it, which did facilitate a modicum of prediction and control. These, today elaborated and refined to great effect, combine observation and empirical sampling with statistical calculation, with a varied use of the theory of probability, and result in congruent manipulations and forecasts. From psychology to economics and politics and sociology and even history, these methods have been much more successful than is recognized.[4]

For the discussion of modern man's problem of freedom, however, the significant event in their story is the taking over of their statistical premises and techniques by the sciences of nature. Modern physics, chemistry, and biochemistry, particularly, have become at least as statistical as

---

[4] See Edmund Brunner, "The Role of the Social Sciences in the American Scene," *Teachers College Record*, vol. XLVII, no. 7, April, 1946; George Lundberg, *Can Science Save Us?* (New York, 1947).

modern sociology. The blueprint of existence [5] with which the new physics provides us signalizes a stuff whose substance is mutability. In one set of determinations it is a particle, in another it is a wave; in either mode it is a quantum, an indeterminately so-much-and-no-more of energy. It eventuates and continues as a variety of recognizable characters; as electrons, protons, positrons, photons, neutrons, neutrinos, and what have you. These compound in an unending variety of ways and in what is still held to be an orderly and measurable progression, making up the different groups of different sizes and shapes and qualities and behaviors called atoms. But every atom consists of an indefinite space wherein swims a sunlike nucleus of protons with one or more planetlike electrons moving around it. Every atom is far more space than stuff, but the stuff it has is terribly powerful. No atom has a determinate boundary and the motions of the electrons within it are such that when we define their position we cannot measure their speed; when we measure their speed we cannot define their position. Principle of indeterminancy is the physicist's name for this elusiveness. Not only do electrons within the atom have their separate and arbitrary motions, the atom as a whole has a motion without direction, without order. This is assimilated to the Brownian movement, and is known as heat motion. It is constitutional, constant, anarchic. It distorts any orderly sequence of relationships between atoms. It contributes to making events in which only a small number of them are involved impervious to any recognizable law.

Thus, the closer we get to the intimate stuffs of existence,

---

[5] See Werner Heisenberg, *The Physical Principles of the Quantum Theory*, tr. by Carl Eckart and Frank C. Hoyt (Chicago, 1930); Erwin Schrödinger, *Science and the Human Temperament*, tr. by James Murphy and W. H. Johnston (New York, 1935); *What Is Life?* (New York, 1945); A. W. Meyer, *The Rise of Embryology* (Stanford, 1939); J. Needham, *Biochemistry and Morphogenesis* (Cambridge, Eng., 1942).

the less repetitive, the less predictable, and hence the less controllable its behavior becomes. To achieve prediction and the control which prediction enables, we must move from the depths to the surface of existence. We must envisage the atoms and their energies in immense numbers, transfinite numbers, and measure them as the social scientist measures social events—statistically. The greater the numbers, the greater the correctness of the measurements and the accuracy of the laws. But since the instruments of measurements are themselves factors in the determination of the measure, the point is reached where the measuring tool becomes itself a part of the measurement. The situation points to the conclusion that true chance underlies necessity: that freedom is the ground of order, and that order is a function of multitude, not solitude. Law supervenes on numbers. Law is not the foundation but the skyline of existence, a consequence and not a cause. The foundation is freedom and law is the organization of freedom.

At the point of initiation of the ordered world then, the point where determinism begins to emerge, determinism can be recognized as a mutual determination of countless diverse liberties; a determination on the average and as a whole. The world of order which the sciences of nature search out, demonstrate, and work on is a small indefinite island of regular sequences more or less equivalent which has freely made itself in an infinite sea of liberties. The world of order is a mutual checking, a locking-up and channeling of indeterminate immense energies of whose potencies we have made for ourselves, in their release through atomic fission, a small, but sufficient sample.

The formation of this island of order has not been instant, nor singular, nor continuous. To experience, indeed, order is a viable archipelago of islands, not a single island. It is a plural process for which the philosopher's word is *duration,* the biologist's *evolution.* The world of law and order lasts; that is, the successive phases of its events which we call present, past, and future do not altogether shut each other out, but more or less interpenetrate as they succeed one another, like the tones in a melody or the words in a sentence. Although they take place, it cannot be said that they occupy space any more than space occupies them. Rather is their shape a reciprocally determining space-time whose differentia is activity, temporality. The stark anatomy of the cosmic process shows a combination of periodic recurrence with aperiodic variation, of repetition and novelty, of continuities and discontinuities, of determinism and freedom. From its inferred beginnings, billions of years ago, the cosmos has developed as a process of divergence by compounding, by spreading like a fan, by bursting in successive bursts like a multiple rocket.

The astronomical physicist further emphasizes the variety, multiplicity, and indeterminateness of original nature and of her processes as the mutual determinations of her parts. These being energies, their inwardness is process, eventuation, passage of time. The methods and the findings of the Einsteinian relativist convert the old Newtonian idea of time which was employed by earlier physics and by recent common sense in the daily business of living, from an original into a resultant, into a configuration derived and not an element given. Original, elemental, are the diverse and singular times of the diverse and singular beings whose coming together—each different from the others and having to be a neighbor to the others—produces the convention of their common time. For today's physics all times are local times; all are compenetrations of space with duration; all are space-times. Save as the self-orchestration of these diversities, there is no one and total time, everywhere

42

the same; nor is there any definite time order between different events in different places, everywhere the same. Things are such events; thoughts are such events. Both are quanta or drops or spaces of duration differentiating, and their divergences are lapses between them—intervals the physicists say—that we analyze and measure by means of a convention of measuring which alters as we change our measuring instruments. It would follow that thoughts and things are neither substances nor grounds but orders of comings and goings. Their differentiae are arrangements and relationships of sequences which pass into and out of each other like the colors of a spectrum or the sonorities of a sound. Also their perceptual inwardness is mobility, diversification, mutually held to measure and persistence by their coming together.

*   *   *

So far, we believe, the present frontier of the fan-spread, the farthermost burst of the rocket, is man. Human nature and existence present themselves as a minuscule, late, precarious, compenetration of the cosmic act—energies into particles, particles into atoms, atoms into molecules, molecules into cells, cells into organisms, organisms into varieties, varieties into species, and species into the behaviors which compose, and composing transform, their nature and existence. Each new phase is a new, unique, unpredictable total event, not foregone in what had gone before. Men are among the most recent such comers to their singularity and difference. At the core of any one of the human species, there are his genes. These are the propulsive multiple rocket of his being. As an event in nature, genes are themselves an extraordinary mutation upon the primal ordered compounds which the physicists and chemists study. The chromosomes of which genes are arrangements are not composed of enough atoms—only a few million each—to supply the material needful for a statistical rule. Yet the atoms which make them up are arranged in such an order that to geneticists, the impulsion, the shape, the growth pattern, and the manifold drives of the organism are already preordained by that order. Let it be the life of a louse or the life of a lady, the genes start it, keep it going, and give it shape. In each thing living they are the plan, the builder, and the building. The structure within them is singular to each individual. Both the initiation of his existence and the sustaining directive of his biography, this structure repeats itself within each cell of his body as unique as his fingerprints. It seems to be the ground and force of the animal assurance which from conception to death carries him over sharp edges of multitudinous dangers that he knows not of. For seed and embryo perish in multitudes to which those who are born and perish are but a handful, and those who are born and grow up and grow old less than a handful to those who die young.[6]

The form of this strict *élan* that only destruction will hold back is an orchestration of two streams of events— carried from a long past by the genes of a man's two parents. Different stages of its intra-uterine progression suggest in some degree adults of lower, less differentiated forms—condensed, compenetrated, hastened recapitulations, such as hocus-pocus is of *hoc est corpus meus*. As it ripens, it becomes a vertebrate which, instead of beak or tooth or claw or snout with single functions set to single tasks, makes itself a cerebral cortex of greater size than any other beast can boast. Between the works of man and this overgrowth of cortex, the authorities see a direct connection. The record shows that Homo sapiens, after he is born, possesses, as compared with any other mammal, an

---

[6] See G. W. Corner, *Ourselves Unborn* (New Haven, 1944).

enormous versatility, an overweening power of awareness, selection, symbolization, and response. The record shows that man can live anywhere, eat anything, move everywhere, do anything, and undo anything.

Darwin's "spontaneous variations" may be attributable to changes of electronic orbit and similar alterations of the patterns in the germ cells. And new species may be the trajectory of the new pattern in the world which the eye can see, the ear hear, and the hand grasp. Such chanceful ruptures and reformations of a foregoing chromosomic order may be the all of purely biological freedom. Once they have come to pass, the mutants repeat themselves indefinitely as the new organism ripens and comes to its animal birth.

Nor is it beyond conjecture that a man's conscious experience of his personal liberty may not be as continuous with this subatomic original as a stream is with its springs. Human freedom may be this authentic irreducible deviation, coming now to pass, not in the simplest and most inward stuff of events, but on their most forward, most intricately compounded and patterned frontier. On either level, there occurs an interplay of repetition and innovation, of necessary connection and undetermined sequence, such that the transforming variant consummates the suffusion of the past by the future which the merely repetitive activity of self-maintenance has failed to accomplish. On the human level, however, every personality struggling to preserve itself alters as it struggles yet sustains its identity. It remains the same only as the sameness keeps failing, for to make the repetitions which are order is not enough; to sustain order it must also supplement repetition with the breach of order which is innovation. It imagines, discovers, invents, creates. Ultimately this liberty is the salvation of order, and order the channel of liberty.

One psychologist, adept in the methods of determinism, accounts for this singularity of Homo sapiens by what he calls "the confirming reaction." I refer to the Nestor of American psychologists, Edward Thorndike. Considering *Man and His Works,* he reviews the dynamics, the mechanism, the methods, and the goals of human conduct. Of the countless items of this conduct, born of the genes and borne by the genes into the acts of speech and the institutions of society, those that establish themselves and grow often do so by virtue of "the confirming reaction." Those that fail sometimes do so because they do not receive "the confirming reaction." This event might be described as a sort of closing click of satisfaction which ensues when an agreeable linkage of some sort has come to pass. It works back upon the connection after it has operated, to strengthen or re-enforce it. Although, says Thorndike, "the confirming reaction" is a part of natural biological causation and performs like a hormone and not like a syllogism, it

may be in some cases the act of a free agent, a free will, in the most useful sense of those words. . . . The environment, . . . the world, . . . undoubtedly determines most of what occurs in man and most of what is rewarded. Most, but not all. . . . The confirming reaction is issued by a man, when that man is satisfied. That man originates as a certain collection or battery or outfit of genes which is by definition and hypothesis apart from and contrasted with its environment. Day by day that man has changed his nature partly by the influence of his own confirmation of connections whose consequences satisfy him. Each person is to that extent an *imperium in imperio naturae.* Each person is a center of creative force modifying himself more or less to suit himself.[7]

---

[7] See Edward L. Thorndike, *Man and His Works* (Cambridge, Mass., 1943), pp. 39–40.

Here, now, is something to look well at. Edward Thorndike is a determinist and a mechanist. His studies of man have been undertakings to discern causal sequence and necessary connections, and to define and measure them with the utmost precision. His connectionist system of psychology has been deprecated, I think quite unfairly, as a clockwork system of human nature. Yet his "confirming reaction" is to a connectional pattern what winding a clock is to the clock. It is the directive and energy-channeling orchestration of one arrangement of energies with another quite different one. As compared with the clock, the winder is free, the clock is determined. The winder may wind or not wind. But the state of the clock must conform to the decision of the winder. So with the "confirming reaction" and the connection it confirms. To make it known to his readers Thorndike spontaneously employs the expressions *creative force, free agent, free will*. Let this force, agent, or will be syllogism or hormone or whatever its godfather prefers, he sees it as free. So far as concerns the stimulus-response mechanism, it comes unnecessarily and superfluously; its coming is neither required nor implied by the sequential associationist mechanics wherein the psychologist's satisfactory connection consists. State its dynamics in an equation, and the energy of confirmation would call for a numeral of indeterminate amount, upsetting and throwing out of balance the neat articulation of the stimulus-response on which it supervenes. It would be a gratuitous figure, for which no fitter word than *free* can be found.

II. THE FREE SOCIETY OF FREE MEN

Having had our quick look at the solutions of the problem of freedom in the modern world which we receive in the

47

images of nature and of original human nature produced
by quantum theory, relativity, genetics, embryology, and
psychology, we are ready to look at the problems of freedom in modern society. They are problems, you will recall,
brought to birth by science, democracy, technics, and
peace as divisions of the human enterprise. All of them are
problems of organization. The base of each, according to
its kind, is stasis. Stasis is what comes to pass when organization hardens in whole or in part into hierarchy, and any of
the diverse movements of human life are halted, dammed
up and immobilized. Then fluent and peaceful action con-
denses into explosive tension which, if not released before
too late, bursts into overt warfare. For each of these departments of modern life, hence, the solution of its problems
would be such an organization of freedom, such a coming
together of human beings in their persons, their ways, and
their works that each would live more freely, more abundantly, and more assuredly than he could if he walked
alone.

Organizations which truly seek—I do not say attain—
this character are free societies. This is their sign: that their
form tends to orchestrate to one another the two freedoms:
libertas obedientiae—the modern world's liberation from
the coercions of nature by the determinism of science and
technics—and creative liberty or free will—any personality's origination, choice, support, and bringing to security
of an innovation, of a new thought, or tool or thing for
which the determinations of the past offer no sanction and
the conditions of the present no friendship. Indeed it might
be said that any problem is a problem of freedom if it can
be solved by such an orchestration of the two freedoms.

Some would argue that the statistical conception of natural law is a solution of this kind, and that a similar solution of the social problem of authority could be reached, if

48

that were re-envisaged as an orchestration of the equal liberty of irreducibly different persons living irreducibly different lives by means of a union of economies and cultures. The union would then operate as both the achievement and channel of personal liberty, as consummation of its products, tools, and production. It would be thus, for the life course of any individual, the arrangement of instrumentalities wherewith the "big, blooming, buzzing confusion" of the undirected, self-extinguishing choices and movements which make up his infancy would transmute into the directive, self-sustaining purposes and actions of his better-patterned maturity. So, his growing would be learning, his learning growing. And his learning would consist in the self-compounding assimilation of new skills and new knowledge, in their suffusing and transforming of his old ways, in their enhancing, diversifying, and recanalizing his old powers. His learning would be an organization of his freedom.

The more varied and viable the culture a child grows up in, the more abundant his choices; the more abundant his choices, the better his chances of correcting and revising his past, and of diversifying and consummating his future; the more successfully he accomplishes this, the more fertile he makes his soil and the more numerous he makes his openings for creation and invention and the richer he makes the field of his "confirming reaction." If the *quale* of freedom is ineffably the spring, its scope and channel is the culture which it created and creates and which in turn feeds it. Orchestration transvalues natural necessity and social authority from masters into servants of personal free will; orchestration promotes *libertas obedientiae* from the harness into the handmaiden of creative liberty.

*　　*　　*

How men of science attain orchestration is an open secret. For orchestration is, and ever has been, the working condition of bona fide science, the ground of its method, and the dynamic of its customs and mores. It is the embodiment and exemplification of the first of the Four Freedoms and the initiation of all the others. You can see it wherever a scientific enterprise is under way and is carried by its own impulsions in its own manner without blocking from church, state, or industry. Let us take for a sample of such an enterprise the research into the causes and healing of cancer. Men and women of all the lands and cultures of the world are embarked on this research. Each has the hope that *he* and not another, may conceive the hypothesis, devise the experimental tests, proclaim the verifications of the cause and cure of cancer. Each is thus the competitor of every other inquirer in the enterprise. Should he achieve his purpose, mankind would crown him with fame and honors and count him great among the greatest heroes and benefactors of the race. Suppose an idea occurs to him—new, unprecedented, without link in the theory and practice of cancer research, and sure to be condemned by the experts. However and wherever it comes to him—while working at something quite different in his laboratory, as an accidental perception during a fishing trip, in a conversation at a cocktail party or during a kiss at a necking party, in a dream or at a meal—it is, as it first comes, a free datum with the ineffable *quale* of freedom. All his past experience, all his present knowledge and his present skill may deny it, cut it off, and shut it out. But he experiences that "slow, dead heave of the will" which constitutes decision *against* his idea's alternatives and *for* his idea. It becomes a belief on which he stakes his reputation and his life. He gives it the accolade of *value.*

What, for him the scientist, is the next step? Is it to proclaim his idea as a doctrine infallible and inalterable, and announce himself, its author, to be the sole authentic authority over every such idea? Is it to indoctrinate others with his own view, and to insist that all experiment must seek to verify that view as a foregone conclusion? Is it, to say to his fellow inquirers and all the world beside: "I am right and you are wrong: you owe me assent and support because I am right. I owe you silencing and suppression because you are wrong."

Can you conceive of a scientist with such an attitude? You cannot. You know that our genius in cancer research would do what every scientist, everywhere in the world, would do. He would take his idea for a working hypothesis. He would set up his experiment not to verify it as foregone conclusion but to test its competency as one more of the alternatives already in the competitive field. He would communicate his idea, his techniques, and his findings to all the inquirers in the field. He would ask them to check on every step of his personal undertaking. He would invite their critical judgments and proffers of alternatives that could do the same job as well or better. He would welcome the alternatives as tests of his hypothesis. He might challenge the routines and rigidities by which experts are known as experts by showing that they are not scientific mobility but unscientific stasis; he, himself, however, would keep to mobility as his own rule. And his fellow inquirers would respond. They would repeat and vary his experiments and check his observations and his arguments, step for step. If after a succession of such checks and verifications, they reached a consensus confirming his hypothesis, this confirmation would change it from a claim to truth into a truth. It would be called by the author's name and bring him his due rewards. Yet it would be anything but his exclusively personal achievement. The labors of every inquirer in the

51

field would have contributed to making it what it had at last become and to endowing it with the authority it now could rightly claim. Each and every one of them by his doubts and dissents no less than by his agreements would have contributed to the realization of the author's hopes and thus the defeat of their own, yet without frustration and without envy.

And is not this generally the case among men of science? The fame of a scientist and the authority of his findings are not simply overflowings of his uniqueness and *expertise*. Both ensue upon the free consensus of his peers and competitors, reached by the methods of careful, free inquiry. Validity accrues to his findings not in virtue of *what* has been found, but in virtue of *how* it has been found. This *how*—the method of science—clearly is an orchestration, a process of co-operative competition and competitive co-operation in which the sanction of the findings accrues from the procedures of finding out. And never, where the method holds which distinguishes scientific from other ways of thinking, can any finding be exempted from the tests and challenges of these procedures.

This is why it is falsely charged that science cannot treat of values. It must be clear, on the contrary, that it is science that treats of values more hopefully and satisfactorily than any of its competitors. For when men approach values in the spirit and by the method of science, the warfare of moral ideals which human history so largely narrates, is turned toward conciliation and peace. Then the stasis by which values are usually set over against one another and against facts is dissolved into a progressive checking of the monopolist pretensions of an ineffable preference or an infallible belief by the effable test of consequences to its own confirmation and survival in a field of equal competition with its peers. Proponents of absolute ideas of right and wrong, of beauty, truth and goodness, ideas of God and immortality; of anarchist, capitalist, socialist, communist, fascist conceptions of human nature and human relations, no less than of the traditional churchly orthodoxies—all with their prescriptions about love and begetting, marriage and divorce, property and power and authority—are, on the record, eager to escape challenge and to evade the checking and testing of equal competition. They insist that their values can neither undergo nor sanction the procedures of science. All the doctrines and disciplines for whose definition and determination today's social sciences vie with yesterday's theology, metaphysics, ethics, and aesthetics deny that values and facts are commensurable or that the method of science has any import for the existence of values. But if they really believed what they claim they would not struggle to shut out and cut off the method of science; since they do struggle, they cannot believe what they say.

The fact is that short of killing or being killed the validation of value consists in some form of discourse. The alternative would be silence. And proponents of values are anything but silent. They are forever proving what they insist is beyond proof. But the proof of that sort of thing is circular. Most discourses about values assume what they set out to prove and argue a foregone conclusion. The method of science, on the other hand, is not circular. It is the form that debate receives when it treats alternative claims as equal and gives each the fullest opportunity to make itself good in consequences. On closer inspection of the relations of values and facts, it turns out that a fact is made a value when someone clings to and cherishes it in spite of consequences, when he declines to risk it on equal terms against the competition of alternatives according to the methods and tests of scientific discourse, whereas, per contra, a value

53

is made a fact when its validity is freely submitted to these validations.

And can anything different be the case with freedom? Is freedom a value beyond proof or a fact whose proof is its consequences? Obviously, we first experience freedom directly as a perceptual event in our personal lives. We have yet to learn *about* it, or whether that first *knowledge-of-acquaintance* can ever receive the predicates of *knowledge-about*. The postulates and procedures of scientific method are the places for gaining this *knowledge-about*. Let them lead to determinations of freedom or let the immediate perceptual event defeat determination; either consequence will bring such *knowledge-about,* and it will be a test and validating of the direct experience. And is not the very use itself of scientific method postulated upon the validity of the experience and the continual test of it? What else, as a social instrument, is the method of science but the art of bringing liberty of conscience, liberty of thought and of expression to power and efficiency? What is the scientific inquirers' organization of these liberties but their association in such a way that each man may go about his business more freely and bravely than he could alone?

Here religion has learned something from science, and the religion of the modern man is postulated on the similar organization of liberty. This is exemplified in such religious societies whose internal pattern and external associations are according to this plan.[8] As among the scientific disciplines, the orchestration of their diversities is a mutual de-

---

[8] The Federal Council of the Churches of Christ in America seems to me to approximate such a free association of free religious societies. The Interfaith movement is an effort in a similar direction. But by and large, the sects and cults of the Judeo-Christian tradition present a great variety of unmollified stases. See Searle Bates, *Religious Liberty—an Inquiry* (New York, 1944).

termination which intensifies and makes safer the liberty it channels. No minority becomes a tyrant, no majority a persecutor. Every doctrine and discipline can undertake in security to make good its claim to excellence by achievement and not by *force majeure,* favor, or privilege: by endeavoring to do the same job better than its competitors. So if it succeeds, its success is a merited success, the success of a champion who meets all comers. If it failed to excel it would not be champion.

But the order and rule of this form of the competition of faiths is the organization of liberty of religion as the method of science.

* * *

That the method of science does accomplish the orchestration of creative liberty and *libertas obedientiae,* of freedom and determinism in the sciences, follows from what it is and the way it works. Its import for the sects and denominations of the religions has not grown to the maturity it promises, but is on its arduous way. If freedom of speech and expression and freedom of worship (which is but freedom of communication with divinity) are to come to men everywhere in the world, they will come only through the fluent co-operative competition and competitive co-operation of whose mutualities scientific method is our most successful configuration.

The perfection and variation of the method have depended, however, not alone on the vision and will of the scientists. They have depended no less on the materials and tools with which vision is embodied, and the instrumentalities whereby vision is communicated and discussed. Without liberty of communication speech is soliloquy, expression shadow. All association is a function of communication, and where its devices have been few and small and weak, social coherence has been biological, limited, institutional, not personal. It was in view of the available agencies of communication that Aristotle would admit no more than 10,000 citizens to his ideal polity.[9] Local and almost total, though not in our sense of the word democratic, autonomies persisted or came into being under even the most efficient of the tyrannical predatory empires. The invention of printing and of ever-swifter automotive vehicles to carry speech and speakers from anywhere on the globe to anywhere else, has enabled the almost instant coming together of human beings in numbers whose actual association was unthinkable a couple of generations ago. Paper and presses, the stuffs and patterns which make up telegraph, telephone, radio, television, radar, the devices of transportation by land, water, or air constitute the circulatory system of the Great Society. They are the efficacious forces in bringing the peoples of the globe into the precarious but hopeful association which has come to be signalized as One World. Thus, a stasis in the functioning of the instruments of communication could stop science and throw back religion. Whoever has power over the instruments of communication has power over the nourishment, the variation, the growth, and the development of science, religion, industry, and art.

Obviously the substance of such power must be economic. Possession and ownership give it; changes in possession and ownership change it. A political or ecclesiastic censor can produce stasis in communication, can distort, cut off, or shut out ideas only as he is master of their channels. These, in our industrial society, are so complex and involve so much capital investment that they are automatically Big Business and soon become monopoly. Complaints have been common of a certain cartelization of communi-

---

[9] See *The Politics*, Books VII, VIII.

cations; repeatedly, public attention has been called to great chains of newspapers and radio networks, to motion-picture trusts, book-publishing corporations. Not infrequently it comes to light that the ideas which are communicated through these instruments are simply those which the owners as managers choose to have communicated. Thus, the modern world adds the industrial monopolist to the older politician and churchman, who, by controlling communication, imposes an artificial economy of scarcity in ideas and makes freedom of speech and expression a problem.[10]

The customary riposte to such control has two forms: one is policing by government which always tends toward complete bureaucratic control. The other is the unionization of workers in the communications industries, which seems to move toward an artificial economy of scarcity in knowledge and skills. Before long, monopoly of instruments of communication is joined by monopoly of man power in communications; the Hearsts of journalism get the Petrillos of the arts for company. But how can stasis in the form of strikes bring relief from stasis in the form of censorship and price fixing? Orchestration here would be such an association of the interests, powers, and functions that are affected in stoppage as would keep the channels of communication open and movement through them free for all ideas on equal terms.

*   *   *

The shaping of such an association is as difficult as the stake of science and the arts in it is great. Its inadequacy would lame them; its failure would stop them in their tracks. But the consideration of it shifts the problem of free-

---

[10] See "Thought Control in America," *Far Eastern Survey*, May 22, 1946.

dom to another no less critical attribute of modernity. We are back at the total problem posed by the structure and operations of industry—its mass production beyond the power to buy though not the ability to consume at home, its resulting struggle for markets abroad, and the cartelizations ensuing. More intimately, we are back at the problem posed by the hierarchical order of authority in industry, by the general producer-consumer schizophrenia in society, by the factory's digestion—via the division of labor—of the individual as producer of finished products, by its resulting frustration of the instinct of workmanship, by its abridgement and depersonalization of workers into machine tenders operating as biological extensions of their machines and attached and laid off at will by managerial authority.

Upon that power of a few men over the support of the many, the trade union and its techniques seem to be a none too reliable check. Union or no union, there rose in the psyche of industrial workers an enduring anxiety about their jobs. This mood sought assuagement by projecting a new right—the right to work. Between the First and the Second World Wars the moral atmosphere of industrial countries became charged with an urge toward security, security meaning first and foremost certainty of employment; and secondly, insurance of the individual by the community from the consequences of disemployment, illness, or old age. The mood overflowed to nonindustrial countries. The idea, as against the experience, of freedom was suppressed by a blind anxiety which chose bondage with certainty of employment rather than freedom with uncertainty of employment. The new tyrannies of Mussolini, Hitler, Dollfuss, and others on the continent of Europe were the fruits of that choice; those of Stalin, Chiang Kai-shek, and Franco have a different root but grow an identical fruit. Whatever the root, the servile state is made a haven from the free society.

Such continues to be the situation which "freedom from want" focalizes. Unmodern man meant no more by "freedom from want" than the freedom from hunger and privation which his own labors could achieve. His emphasis was consumption. Modern man means by it freedom from the power of another over his own support. His emphasis is production. Neither our American Declaration of Independence nor the French Declaration of the Rights of Man and the Citizen envisages the security which moderns crave. The impact of that craving on the organization of liberty may be gathered from the Preamble of the Constitution of the Fourth French Republic, adopted the other day by the individualistic French people. The preamble reaffirms the "Principles of 1789" and then supplements them, "as particularly necessary in our time" with "political, economic and social principles" among which are "the duty to work and the right to obtain employment," union membership, collective bargaining, education, and security, the repudiation of War, and the affirmation of international law.[11]

---

[11] As reported in the New York *Times* of Sept. 20, 1946, the preamble to the new French constitution reads as follows:

On the morrow of the victory of the free people over the regimes that attempted to enslave and degrade the human person, the French people proclaims again that every human being, without distinction of race, religion or belief, possesses inalienable and sacred rights. It solemnly reaffirms the freedoms of man and of the citizen consecrated by the declaration of rights of 1789 and the fundamental principles recognized by the laws of the Republic.

It proclaims, moreover, as particularly necessary in our time, the following political, economic and social principles.

The law guarantees to women in all domains equal rights with those of man.

Anyone persecuted because of his acts in favor of liberty has the right of asylum on the territories of the Republic.

The impression is inescapable that affirmative liberty, freedom *for*—in 1789 "the power of doing what does not injure another"—is less momentous than negative security, freedom *from*. Emphasis falls upon work, production. And this continues to be the supreme value, precious, ineffable, of every industrial land and of every land whose public purpose is industrialization. The good society would be a society where jobs are more numerous than men, where there is full employment and everybody's working, everybody's producing. This millennial state had had its brief day during the late fighting which the present War of Words continues, when even the very young and the very old worked and produced and there still were not workers enough. But during the fighting war, production was a means, not an end. The end was victory over the foe, and production was set to the procurement of victory. Govern-

Everyone has the duty to work and the right to obtain employment. No one may suffer in his work or his employment by reason of his origins, his opinions or his beliefs.

Every man may defend his rights and interests by trade-union action and may join the union of his choice.

The right to strike is exercised within the framework of the laws that govern it.

Every worker, through his delegates, participates in collective bargaining on working conditions as well as in the management of business.

All property and all business whose exploitation has acquired the characteristics of a national public service or a monopoly in fact should become the property of the community.

The nation assures to the individual and to the family the conditions necessary to their development.

It guarantees to all, and notably to the child, to the mother and to aged workers, protection for health, material security, rest and leisure.

Every human being who, by reason of his age, physical or mental condition or economic situation, finds himself incapable of work has the right to obtain from the community the means of decent living.

The nation proclaims the solidarity and equality of all French citizens with regard to the burden resulting from national calamities.

The nation guarantees equal access of the child and the adult to in-ment, the all-powerful agency of this procurement, became the insatiable customer. It set the standards of the goods it wanted, and meticulously and in detail laid the specifications down of what they should be made of, how they should be made, and for what price. It accumulated enormous surpluses of all kinds. If abundance for it meant scarcity for the citizens, that was to be accepted and endured. Excess might be waste, but excess was the insurance of victory. War is forever the ultimate consumer. It can be fought to victory only by preponderant force, all its resources must be expendable, and excess is the dynamic of preponderance. The victor may be spent by the battle, but he has had more of what it takes than the vanquished.

When the war is won—or lost—the all-demanding customer disappears from the scene as buyer; surplus commodities become an issue of the market. Fighting men come back to seek peace-time occupations; employees of war-grown factories are laid off. People also become surplus. Men and women are on their own again. Anxiety

---

structional training and to culture. The organization of free and secular public education at all stages is a duty of the state.

The French Republic, faithful to its traditions, conforms to the rules of international law. It will undertake no war with a view to conquest and will never employ its forces against the liberty of any people.

On condition of reciprocity, France consents to the limitations of sovereignty necessary to the organization and defense of peace.

France forms with the peoples overseas a union founded on the equality of rights and duties without distinction of race or religion.

The French Union is composed of nations and peoples placing in common, or coordinating, their resources and their efforts to develop their civilization, to increase their well-being and to assure their security.

Faithful to her traditional mission, France proposes to guide the peoples for whom she has assumed responsibility toward freedom to govern themselves and democratically to manage their own affairs; putting aside all systems of colonization founded on arbitrary power, she guarantees to all access to public office and the exercise of the individual or collective rights and liberties proclaimed or confirmed above.

about security again makes itself felt. Now industry takes over. Instead of the consumer imposing the standard of production, the producer devises his own specifications and connives in the market to get as much and give as little as he can. The course of the world's various industrial economies since the fighting stopped, with their false scarcities, their bitter struggles over surpluses, prices, wages, and public controls gives us the consequences. The gospel of salvation by "production," "full employment," "60,000,000 jobs" is then preached even more vociferously.

But hardly anybody pauses to inquire, production for whom? employment for what end? For certainly production cannot be taken as an end in itself. The *crises pléthoriques*, the stases of the business cycle, are the disasters which ensue when men think of themselves merely as producers and produce to produce and not to consume. Consumption holds a biological and moral as well as an economic priority over production. Consumption is not only the spendings of night life for whose sake industrial man accumulates the earnings of day life; consumption is every free expenditure of a man's personal energies through the exercise and diversification of his personal faculties. Whenever and wherever a man can work freely and willingly and wisely, so that he validates his labor with "the confirming reaction," production becomes consumption.

This observation gives the idea of full employment a new quality. It turns the notion of security in a different direction. Both have considerable import for freedom in the industrial economy. For when a man works willingly, freely, and wisely, so that the consummations of night life suffuse the activities of day life, labor has become coterminous with leisure, and the producer-consumer split of the personality has been healed. Let it be remembered that *gentlemen of leisure*, with incomes which enable them to live without working, suffer neither self-reproach nor social disapproval for being jobless and unemployed. On the contrary, they are the Joneses with whom *labor* aspires to keep up. They may be far busier than any busy wage earner. It is the freedom of their performance, not its matter or manner nor even its prestige or social importance which signalizes it as leisure against the others' labor. What else, for example, distinguishes the archaeologist from the garbage collector? Each collects garbage—the archaeologist dead, the garbage collector living, garbage. If archaeologists disappeared from modern society, its works and ways would in no way be disturbed. But if garbage collectors merely went on a brief strike, the economy of their community would be seriously menaced. Garbage collecting is an occupation of high social significance and no prestige. Archaeology is an occupation of high prestige and no social significance. Yet who would choose to be a garbage collector if he could be an archaeologist? For archaeology is a free activity wherein diverse knowledge and skills orchestrate with unpleasant sheer physical labor. Garbage collecting figures as solely unpleasant physical labor disgusting to others. Some would appraise prostitution in the same way—a gainful employment of high social significance and no prestige, cutting its workers off and shutting them out. Orchestrate the exclusively sexual relation to others of which women are capable, omit considerations of price, and the prostitute is transvalued into an Aspasia, a Poppaea, a Du Barry, a Maintenon, or a Josephine.

The point of all this is that no normally healthy person can do without employment, that the employment he can't do without must bring "the confirming reaction," that a lead toward the confirming reaction is social participation and social approval. The amount of money a job brings is not of first importance, nor is its material function.

63

What is of first importance is that a man fulfills himself in it and grows through it. Idleness is intolerable because it is emptiness. When you try to bring down that which recent discussion makes so much of as the "infinite dignity and worth of the individual" to the actualities of personal experience, you find that for the individual himself, it amounts to his awareness of his powers in action, growing and diversifying through action. These are his "life, liberty and pursuit of happiness." They are, that is, his awareness of an orchestration within, of his creative liberty and his *libertas obedientiae.* His occupation, to bring him this awareness, must give him a life as well as a living.

What this means for the organization of liberty in industry is in no way different from the organization of liberty in science. As studies begun more than a quarter of a century ago prove,[12] it means on the producer side the citizenship of the worker in the industry; it means the spontaneous team play and the full participation of the individual in the group; it means that *Industry* holds no secrets from *Labor,* but all share completely the knowl-

[12] See Chester Barnard, *The Functions of the Executive* (Cambridge, Mass., 1938); J. B. Fox and J. F. Scott, *Absenteeism: Management's Problem* (Boston, 1943); Alfred Marrow, "Pajamas and the Ego," *Fortune* magazine, Aug., 1946; Elton Mayo, "Revery and Industrial Fatigue," *Personnel Journal,* Dec., 1924; *The Human Problems of an Industrial Civilization* (New York, 1933); *The Social Problems of an Industrial Civilization* (Boston, 1945); F. J. Roethlisberger and W. J. Dickson, *Management and the Worker* (Cambridge, Mass., 1940); F. J. Roethlisberger, *Management and Morale* (Cambridge, Mass., 1942); Ronald Lippitt, *An Experimental Study of the Effect of Democratic and Authoritarian Group Atmospheres* (in Studies in Topological and Vector Psychology, I, Iowa City, 1940); Kurt Lewin and Alex Bavelas, "Training in Democratic Leadership," *Journal of Abnormal and Social Psychology,* vol. XXXVII, pp. 115–119, Jan., 1942; Alex Bavelas, "Morale and the Training of Leaders," in *Civilian Morale* (New York, 1942); Kurt Lewin, "The Special Case of Germany," in *Public Opinion Quarterly,* Winter, 1943; "The Dynamics of Group Action," in *Educational Leadership,* Jan., 1944.

edge and skills on which the life and growth of the industry depends. It means the dissolution of industrial hierarchy into that form of mobility which will impattern the optimum of co-operative competition and competitive co-operation. It means the transmutation of authority from unconditional directive to viable consensus, communicated through the duly constituted executive. It means the projection of similar relationships beyond the plant to the entire industry in which it figures, beyond the industry to the national and foreign economies in which it trades.

Failing such grass-roots conversion and its extension, freedom becomes an ever more aggravated problem. Where the conversion is achieved security follows, in the one sense in which security can have any lasting value. This is psychological. The richest and most powerful gentlemen of leisure, the steadiest workingmen forever sure of their jobs, may feel equally insecure; and again, a poor tramp, unemployed, never knowing where his next meal will come from, may feel entirely secure. For amid the changes and chances of the industrial economy guarantees are ruled out. They are not observations of fact but projections of faith. Security is peace of mind, and peace of mind comes to any person who feels that his own powers freely employed in teamwork with his neighbors continue and enlarge his own life.

Choose such a conversion for your economic faith and the expression "freedom from want" gets a fresh dynamic. One could free oneself from want like the Buddha, by wanting only to be free of wanting; or again by wanting nothing more and nothing different from what one has. This, however, is not what modernity means by freedom from want. Modernity means a program, not of maintaining a standard of living but of raising standards of living—everywhere in the world. Modernity means thinking up and working out positive plans for a global economy of abundance in whose execution all the peoples of the world might agree to participate. Modern man holds that the satisfaction of existing wants does not raise a standard of living. The coolies of China, the peasants of Russia, the untouchables of India, the peons of the South Americas, and the hillbillys of the North American South live more narrowly and poorly than the tramp and casual worker of industrial cities; if they could enjoy a little more of what they already have, they would be satisfied. But this would not raise their standard of living. To raise a standard of living is to change it. It is to diversify old wants and add new ones, to devise the instruments by which they can be satisfied, and so to employ them that the goods and services which ensue are not merely products but consummations alike for the maker of his makings and the user of his usings. An expanding economy, thus, is one of wants multiplying and diversifying; in it the dynamic of "freedom *from* want" is freedom *to* want ever more goods, and ever more varied goods, spiritual and material. This *wanting* is the entire dynamic, is both the going and the goal of an economy of abundance. In it *getting* or *owning* is a lodging for the night, not a home. "You can't take it with you" bespeaks the wisdom of the free; always, men save what they spend, and lose what they save. This is the law of life for the flesh and the spirit alike.

Obviously, where producers and their singular ends dominate, such a consummation of the law is extremely unlikely. The members of any and every skill, every craft, and every profession are but a handful when set beside the multitudes the satisfaction of whose wants calls into existence the production and the products of the occupational minorities. Members of each such minority in their turn become members of the consumer multitudes when they spend what they earn. The interests of each member as consumer are free interests; they are far more numerous and varied than his interest as producer. Yet while both industry and labor are highly organized and their organization is deeply implicated with the stases of the business cycle, the consumers, for the most part, merely cry to government, and here and there come together in consumer societies. Now, wartime government practice has shown that it is when the consumer holds direct power over production, when he can develop wants and can set the standards and make the specifications for the goods and services to satisfy his wants, that his freedom functions and his self-dependence flourishes. Thus the organization of freedom in industrial society calls for its conversion from a producer to a consumer economy, alike in the phases of making and selling and in the phases of buying and using. It calls for basing the economic organization of freedom on the primacy of the consumer.

*   *   *

Can government be the vehicle of such a shift of base and such a conversion? Socialist dogma answers, *Yes*. The record of democratic governments answers, *No*. The record of totalitarian governments answers emphatically, *No*. Here the crucial instance is not Nazi Germany nor Fascist Italy, nor clerico-fascist Spain; the crucial instance is Communist Russia. Those others built their tyrannies upon the religion of authoritarianism, and their works but embodied and imposed their faiths. Communism, however, came as a religion of liberty and liberation, not only as it was prophesied by Proudhon, but as it was promulgated by Marx, significantly as it was promulgated by Marx. The Soviet power holders have made of it a rationalization of tyranny and enslavement. They employ its principles as a compensation for their practices, so that in Russia, Communism is to the Soviets what in Spain Christianism is to the Falange. Authority is centralized and hierarchical and is supported by an omnipotent secret police: all men are associated in compulsory organizations; their energies are harnessed in the prescriptive actions of "five year plans" of production without consumption and again production; millions are held in concentration camps, for life condemned to be the merest tools with life in them; ideas are under government censorship; communications are under absolute government control; the variant is doomed and suppressed; industry, the arts, the sciences are subjected to periodic purges which remove every potential alternative to the power and views of the power holders.[13] Submission is the price of survival for the Russian multitudes; fear and the cruelties which fear engenders, for the masters of those multitudes. By the providence of the ineluctable Dialectic the means to freedom must be the uttermost negation of freedom; the end justifies the means. The entire condition is sanctified as "building Socialism."

The *No* to governments, in democracies, is constitutive. It is of the very nature of democratic societies. It was the dynamic of the democratic revolution in America and in France. Most of the history of political liberty is a history of a progressive limitation of the powers of the government, of a separation of its legislative, judicial and executive agencies, and of their orchestration as an order of mutual checks and balances.

Counter to this gradient of political change has been the movement of the industrial economy toward centralization and monopoly. This has diverted democratic govern-

---

[13] See Victor Kravchenko, *I Chose Freedom* (New York, 1945); House Document 754, *Communism in Action in the Soviet* (Washington, 1946); "Blue Print for World Conquest," *Human Events* (Chicago, 1946).

ment from its initial path to one which tended to unite the divided powers, and to nationalize controls. It strengthens the central government at the expense of the local and regional governments, and thus ever more contracts the individual's liberties and diminishes the scope of his self-rule and self-help. Their place is taken by bureaucracies.

Vigilance against bureaucracies is a permanent component of the democratic tradition. The state, John Mill wrote in 1859,[14] absorbs through the civil service "the most intelligent and instructed persons procurable," who in due course may become "a numerous bureaucracy to whom alone the rest of the community would look for all things: the multitude for direction and dictation in all they had to do; the able and aspiring for personal advancement."

But when Mill was writing industry had not yet reached its monopolistic growth and the cartel was not even a fantasy. Today industry is a piecemeal fascism, with tremendous power over scientific research, over man's labor as a producer and his liberties as consumer. Today it calls for powers of government so great and so mobilized as to be able to overrule financial oppression and industrial tyranny.[15] Our time is a critical phase of this new form of the struggle for freedom, which carries also a new menace to freedom at its heart. In 1859, Mill was able to say, correctly, that the Americans of his generation were "a people accustomed to transact their own business"; that consequently they have leaders for

every kind of civil business; let them be left without a government, every body of Americans is able to improvise one, and to carry on that or every other kind of public business with a suf-

---

[14] John Stuart Mill, *On Liberty.*
[15] See Gardner Means, *The Structure of the American Economy* (Washington, D.C., 1939–40); Adolf Berle and Gardner Means, *The Modern Corporation and Private Property* (New York. 1933).

69

ficient amount of intelligence, order and decision. This is what every free people ought to be; and a people capable of this is certain to be free; it will never let itself be enslaved by any man or body of men because these are able to seize and pull the reins of the central administration.

Does this continue to hold of the descendants of the men of 1859? There are many—mostly identified with the strivings of monopoly—who mourn that it does not. The New Deal, especially, they say, has amply realized John Mill's worst fears. Others—and they far outnumber the mourners—say that it does, and that the New Deal has further implemented the democratic process of ever wider and more varied orchestrations of self-help and self-rule. They point especially to the policies and procedures of the Departments of the Interior, Agriculture, Labor, and Commerce, submitting intentions to the study and consensus of those whom the intention affected. They point to the release of energies of artists and men of letters,[16] the growth of faith, and work toward the orchestration of diverse cultures into the singularity of American culture. They point to the miracle of mutation of the national economy from one geared to peace to one geared to war. And they point to the T.V.A.[17]

T.V.A. is the *experimentum crucis*. The whole world has its eyes on the T.V.A., for nearly all of our modern problems of freedom are taken for solution together by T.V.A. It has become a world-wide symbol of man's power over himself and over his environment as both the means and ends of freedom. Science, technics, democracy, social peace were purposely shaped into a configuration to channel the

---

[16] See H. M. Kallen, *Art and Freedom* (New York, 1942), vol. II, book XI, ch. xxxi.

[17] See David Lilienthal, *T.V.A.; Democracy on the March* (New York and London, 1944).

liberties of men for their greater freedom. They were brought as knowledge and as skill to men where they lived and as they were, that they might employ these for themselves together and separately according to their needs and desires. The first principle was that the people of the Tennessee Valley should choose them because they wanted to, freely, not accept them necessarily, because they had to. The material and technological point of departure for this choosing was the mastery of the waters of the Tennessee River. The series of twenty-six mighty dams by which its flow is checked and the engines wherewith it is channeled have translated a natural force which had been all waste and danger into wealth and safety. It is 650 miles now of safe waterway for freight from Knoxville in Tennessee to Paducah in Kentucky. Its flow produces electricity for more than 600,000 homes in seven states, and for offices and factories, new and old. Behind the dams that hold its waters back, the shores of the waters held have become the holiday playgrounds of the people. During the 13 years of T.V.A.'s formation and use the Authority as employer and its tens of thousands of employees have handled all issues between them by joint consultation seeking a consensus. In the entire period there has been hardly anything that could be called a strike.

To those who knew the Tennessee Valley 15 years ago and see it now, the people of the Valley are a people reborn. Fifteen years ago their lands were submarginal, their bodies sick, their spirits low and mean, their ignorance and skill-lessness abysmal. They were bondsmen of politicians and quacks and moneylenders. In view of inner and outer obstructions to learning, their turn from this unfreedom is a genuine revolution, unviolent, secure. The directive for any one man's turn is not a ruling but a neighborly example. Farmers with the knowledge and skills of scientific agriculture set the pace by doing, not by talking. Instruction is given only as it is asked for. Since education, to be effective, has to be self-education, self-education it is under T.V.A. Co-operatives flourish and multiply. Rural communities that never had them before, now upon their own initiative and responsibility have telephones, libraries, health centers, schools. The people eat better, drink better, dress better, live in better houses, pursue more diversified interests and activities than they themselves did fifteen years ago, and than their neighbors do now. Compared with their own past, their standard of living is positively higher; and relatively higher by comparison with the present of the better neighboring regions. The boundary between their producer and consumer functions has dissolved. The way to their full orchestration is still long, but the people of the valley are more definitely whole men and free men. Before T.V.A. they did not exemplify Mill's notion of the American. Now they do. May it not be that in the directive which enabled T.V.A. there is embodied a mode of the organization of liberty which government can enchannel and ensure throughout our land? Or any land? For what is the ultimate function of T.V.A. as an instrument of democratic government? It is to enable the peoples of whom and for whom it is the government to grow into, and to exercise fully, their powers of self-help, self-rule, and self-expression, alike in voluntary teamplay and in solitude. It is to build the road, and to regulate the travel of men and associations of men to this end, to see to it that none takes unfair advantage of the common rule or commits trespass upon the right of way of another. Where these things happen on a highway, traffic snarls, vehicles pile up, movement stops, freedom stops, wreckage and disaster come and go on. Good roads, traffic rules, traffic lights, traffic cops are facilitation of equal freedom, the *sine qua non* of mobility. Where these function correctly, everybody—the gargantuan truck, and T model

Ford, the tanklike bus and the boxlike Austin—moves more freely, safely, and quickly on its own way than it could without them. Such is democratic government to the travelers on life's way. And such, by and large, is T.V.A. to the peoples of the Valley. It keeps life's ways open and life's movement free and sure.

*   *   *

The image of democratic government as road maker and road guard is as apt for peace between nations as for freedom within nations. For the consensus which could enact international law and the procedures which could so administer it that an organization of the nations should be government *of* the peoples, *by* the peoples, *for* the peoples, hence an organization of freedom, must be able to facilitate and enforce exactly that rule of oneself and regard for the rights of others to which sovereignty opposes its intransigent veto. The present phase of the searching and seeking for such a consensus began with the Atlantic Charter, moved on via the proclamations of the Four Freedoms and the succession of conferences and organizations of which the United Nations and the United Nations Educational, Scientific and Cultural Organization are currently the high points. All are postulated upon the principle which regulates traffic on the open road. All assume, not only that peoples, states, cultures, occupations, and religions which are different from each other can live together with each other more freely and abundantly than if they went on their own; there is a disposition in all to accord personal liberty international status, and to write into every instrument of international government a bill of individual human rights.[18]

---

[18] See the *Statement of Essential Human Rights* (Americans United, New York, 1945) drafted by an international committee drawn from representatives of legal and other groups in the United States, Great Britain,

Nevertheless, an insurmountable obstruction to the orchestration of mankind festers at the very heart of power in international organization. This is the Security Council whose task it is to police the worldways and keep movement free and safe from war. The Security Council is the

Canada, China, France, Republican Germany, Italy, India, the Latin Americas, Poland, Soviet Russia, and Republican Spain. The chairman of the drafting committee was William Draper Lewis, director of the American Law Institute. The Statement consists of eighteen articles with brief comments on each. One or another has been incorporated in some form in one or another instrument of international organization, from the Charter of the United Nations to the Constitution of UNESCO. Some have been incorporated in certain peace treaties—notably that with Rumania, although the spokesmen for Russia as well as for Rumania protested. The intent of all of them could be achieved by implementing two rules which could be added by amendment to the Charter of the United Nations. The rules are:

First, that no state a member of the United Nations, shall retain or enact any laws which penalize any individual or group on the ground of sex, race, religion, political opinion, occupation or aliency; that all human beings shall be equal before the law of state.

Second, that individuals or groups believing themselves penalized shall have the right to seek redress before an international tribunal established for this purpose.

The likelihood of such amendment is, of course, very, very remote. It is an obvious challenge to sovereignty. It strikes totalitarian organization at the root. Such traditionally handicapped groups as Negroes in North America and South Africa, Hindus in South Africa, Jews everywhere in the Christian world, Protestants in Catholic-dominated countries, traditional religionists in countries with untraditional religions like Communism or Nazism, would be freed by it from their enforced isolation amid their privileged neighbors and their discriminatory governments. In addition to the appeal to human decency and fair play, they would have as a recourse a judicial process of inquiry and judgment; with compulsory world-wide publication of the tribunal's findings. The tribunal would become—as American courts have become for the voluntary association called the American Civil Liberties Union—the institutional world-base for voluntary action by an International Civil Liberties Union or a Global League for the Rights of Man.

The "stateless," such as before the late fighting war could receive only the dubious protection of the Nansen passport, would gain a healthier feeling of security, and the solution of the grievous problem of the Dis-

74

formally designated guardian of the Fourth Freedom, and it may not do its work if one of a few strong states composing it says Veto. That the power which first and most frequently used its Veto is an authoritarian state with a totalitarian economy projects a problem of freedom.

---

placed Persons would be shifted to a sounder ground. Such notable miscarriages of justice as the judicial murder of Sacco and Vanzetti or the persecution of the Scottsboro boys would be a little less likely.

The rights of asylum would receive a validity beyond the mere sufferance of the government of the land of refuge. The new French constitution makes a bold affirmation of this right. But its acid test will be the attitude of the Fourth Republic toward the multitudes of Spaniards in French concentration camps whose one crime was their loyalty to democratic government in their own country. Article 129 of the Soviet Constitution of 1936 provides expressly for asylum to foreign citizens, "persecuted for the defense of the interests of the toilers or scientific activity or for a struggle for national liberation." But the tale of what the Politburo has done to non-Communists, Poles and Jews and Yugo Slavs, to say nothing of men and women of many other nationalities who struggled for national liberation will not bear the telling.

Clearly, in this issue national laws are not enough; domestic good will is not enough. The impact of global public opinion is needed. The force of international sanctions is needed. True, these might little affect the states whose anarchic sovereignty is a function of their power, and whose power enables them to override all reasonableness with a veto. But the multitudes of little states whose weakness can be strengthened only by co-operation with their equals—co-operation with the strong could, on the record, only take the form of submission to the strong— would stand to gain both inward strength and outer status if sanctions are rightly conceived and administered.

Never, in the past, so far as I know, have sanctions been rightly conceived and administered. They have been conformed to the notion that men and states are moved more surely by fear of punishment than by hope of reward. But this idea is rather a projection of the aggressive pleasure of the punisher than the result of experience of any true change in the punished. The experimental evidence of scientific psychology, accumulated over more than half a century, establishes the fact that punishing the action which the punisher does not desire cannot be assumed to confirm the action which the punisher does desire; that punishment is more likely to intensify the fear and hatred of the punisher than to clinch any inclination to satisfy his wishes. In order to move another to do as one likes, one must move the other to like what he does.

75

Can two societies whose faiths and works are as different from each other as the United States and Russia live together with each other so that each would live better than it could alone?

For the Russian veto operates not only on decisions be-

The action one likes must be satisfying to the other. Enacting it must increase the latter's sense of independence, self-help, and well-being; it must evoke "the confirming reaction." This means that sanctions should envisage reward before they envisage punishments. It means that they should be first modes of orchestration, and only when those fail modes of stasis. As Thorndike writes, discussing the psychology of punishment in *Man and His Works,* "International cooperation to remedy international injustices, to ensure the weak equal rights with the strong, and to prevent strife, by international law, international courts, and international police, is then estimable. But international cooperation to prevent national crimes by directing the energies of nations into desirable activities and rewarding these activities is better."

If we understand these rewards to be, as they must, steps in the organization of freedom, then they could be given in the form of duly defined and publicly awarded enhancements of the power, influence, honor, and opportunities of states as they extend the scope and degree of democratic government in civic rule and business undertakings, as they widen and deepen the educational opportunities of their peoples, raise their standard of living, and by liberating trade in thoughts and things grow toward an economy of spiritual and material abundance. In 1919, when the form of the League of Nations was still undecided, I drew up one of the constitutions for the League which was offered to the *peace makers* of the time for consideration. I later published it in the book, *The League of Nations Today and Tomorrow.* The first two articles of this draft read as follows:

I. The purpose of the League of Nations shall be (1) to assure to its members and their peoples security, freedom, equality of economic and of cultural opportunity and to maintain lasting peace. (2) To create and maintain whatever agencies may effect these ends.

II. All states shall be eligible to membership in the League of Nations on the following basis—(1) organization, political and economic; (2) resources, economic and military—actual, not potential; (3) democracy and responsibility of government; (4) literacy of the population; (5) size of the population.

The purpose was first to equate voting strength with ability to cooperate effectively in the work of the League; second, to keep relationships mobile in such a way that any state's road to power and influence

76

fore the Security Council. The government of Russia has stood aside from the financial organization, the relief undertakings, the educational organization, the plan to control the use of atomic energy, and many other programs of international co-operation. It keeps communication between the Russian people and the rest of the world a one-way street. It makes genuine collaboration and teamplay very unlikely.[19] It chooses to walk alone with a train of weak and small peoples that are within easy reach of its_ might, against their own needs and desires, to do its bidding in international affairs.

There are those who hold that free societies and authoritarian societies will, in the nature of things, cut each other off and shut each other out.[20] This is not true. It is not true of free societies which would cease to be free if they ob-

---

in the League would be the betterment of its people's organization, self-government, and culture, and their increase in numbers. With the international scene as it then was, the United States scored highest on the scale and China lowest. Little Switzerland and little Belgium stood many points above Russia. And these relationships would undergo orderly change with changes in the political and cultural economies of the member states. The international organization would, by due rewards, maintain and encourage mobility; it would prize progress in freedom, whereas regression would simply punish itself. Some such tendency arises and continues spontaneously in the relations between states. The thing is to cultivate these natural growths of society as the scientific farmer cultivates the natural growths of the soil.

[19] The consumer co-operatives of Russia are not autonomous voluntary societies organized to last; they are instruments of government policy designed for a purpose, and exist on sufferance. Thus, when the 1946 Congress of the International Cooperative Alliance voted to set up an International Cooperative Petroleum Association, the Russians abstained from voting, since such an Association would also bring the oil reserves of Russia, Rumania, and Hungary under the purviews of the United Nations. The Russians were quite ready to share with the rest of the world goods owned by the rest of the world but were utterly unwilling to share goods owned or controlled by Russia with the rest of the world.

[20] See Harold D. Lasswell, *World Politics Faces Economics* (New York and London, 1945).

structed or forbade the free movement and free communications of their members anywhere in the world. It is not true of authoritarian societies who trust that their doctrine and discipline can prevail on their merits and hence do not require the support of any other than the power of those merits. This is why the peoples of Catholic or autocratic states enjoy at least a limited mobility among non-Catholic thoughts and an extensive mobility among non-Catholic things. It is where power holders do not really believe that the doctrines with which they rationalize their power can convince that they shut out the competition of alternatives which free movement and free communication naturally bring. It is where they lack faith in the superior merit of their own ways and works that they must either shut out the competitor and cut him off or must kill him or be killed by him.

If it be true that an article in the Stalinist credo (this is a reform of the original communist gospel) is that capitalism and communism-a-la-Russe cannot live in the same world together, then Stalinism is aggression against non-Stalinism from its very roots; then keeping the peace with the Politburo cannot be what peace usually is—a process of compromise, of mutual concession and conciliation, adherence will require such an accumulation of preponderant force to an equitable pact. Then keeping the peace with Russia through a union of the nations, in which Russia would not be a member playing an anti-co-operative role, that the Soviet hierarchy would not dare aggression.

If such an international organization of free societies could be sustained, time then would work toward an all-inclusive confederation of the nations and an all-inclusive structure of lasting peace in which Russia would at last be a co-operator. Time would do so because science and technology are such by nature that free communication is life and isolation is death. In the modern world a society effectively shut in and cut off could only repeat its past; it could neither diversify nor enrich its works and ways. Isolation, spiritual or physical or both, dooms it to the atrophies of starvation. Peoples that have tasted alternatives seek them out, at least to test them further. The peoples of Russia are no exception. The iron curtain is an ancient device of tyranny which the power holders of Russia employ against their own people, and its fruits do not commend it either to tyrants or their victims. The pulses of freedom in men's innermost natures may be subatomic in size and unutterably below the threshold of perception in force. But they are inveterate; they do spring eternal. Generation after generation, among all the peoples of the world, they orchestrate into wholes greater than the sum of their parts, and soon or late they overthrow the tyrannies that rein and ride them, to move on at last upon ways of their own making and in companies of their own choosing.

III. THE MAKING OF AN INTERNATIONAL MIND

The steps in which this comes to be, everywhere upon the globe, may be interpreted as phases of the formation of an international mind. Some are events in the nature of things. They happen contingently and accidentally, like any genuine innovation created by man, and then they spread consequentially, in varying spans and tempos, until at last every society in the world may own a replica. This is sometimes called "the diffusion of culture." Others are configurations of expression of instincts achieving consummation; they are different forms of production and product whose similar bases already exist, everywhere in the world. Others are conscious ideals which join the chanceful and the instinctive in a design for an orchestration of liberties that shall be a means to itself as end.

Very shortly before Franklin Roosevelt died he had dictated sentences for a speech which he did not live to deliver. One of these sentences formulates the problem for whose solution these ideals are devised. "Today," the late President had said, "we are faced with the preeminent fact that if civilization is to survive, we must cultivate the science of human relationships—the ability of all peoples, of all kinds, to live together and to work together, in the same world, at peace." He had been at Yalta and at Teheran. He knew. But perhaps it was not so clear to him that the science of these desirable relationships is the science of freedom, and that the science of freedom is the equipment of the international mind.[21]

Need it be argued that the mind of science is an international mind? On the contrary, the entire theory and

[21] The Preamble to the Constitution of the United Nations Educational, Scientific and Cultural Organization restates this observation of the late president clearly and movingly. I set it down here. Of course, that the means can serve the end or that their inevitably gargantuan costs can or will be met is far from a foregone conclusion. The important thing is to have faith but not illusions, and to risk action on this faith.

The Governments of the States Parties to this Constitution on behalf of their peoples declare that since wars begin in the minds of men, it is in the minds of men that the defences of peace must be constructed; that ignorance of each other's ways and lives has been a common cause, throughout the history of mankind, of that suspicion and mistrust between the peoples of the world through which their differences have all too often broken into war; that the great and terrible war which has now ended was a war made possible by the denial of the democratic principles of the dignity, equality and mutual respect of the doctrine of the inequality of men and races; that the wide diffusion of culture, and education of humanity for justice and liberty and peace are indispensable to the dignity of man and constitute a sacred duty which all the nations must fulfil in a spirit of mutual assistance and concern; that a peace based exclusively upon the political and economic arrangements of governments would not be a peace which could secure the unanimous, lasting and sincere support of the peoples of the world, and that the peace practice of scientism—as one college president miscalls its spirit and enterprise—would fall, if it were not an international mind. There is hardly a scientist, even in Germany, even in Russia, who is not eager to tell the world of his peers what he has found out and how, and what he thinks, and to hear from them what they have found out and think. Each man of science, in his laboratory, in his study, and in his classroom is a crossroads center for his field. Unless the streams of inquiry from all the world met in his mind, unless in his mind, they took a new turn and flowed out again to the minds of his peers, he could not be faithful to his chosen task. Scientific societies and journals are arrangements to ease and assure this meeting of minds, and there is no branch of science which lacks its international forums and journals.

What is true of science is no less true of its elder brothers—letters and the arts. There is no merely autochthonous literature or painting or sculpture or poetry. All are cross-fertilized. All are hybrids. All carry the effects of diffusion in their stuff and build; all are foci of diffusion of the singularity of their own stuff and build. Their dynamic is a network of intercommunication and the life of any is a

---

must therefore be founded, if it is not to fail, upon the intellectual and moral solidarity of mankind.

For these reasons, the States parties to this Constitution believing in full and equal opportunities for education for all, in the unrestricted pursuit of objective truth, and in the free exchange of ideas and knowledge, are agreed and determined to develop and to increase the means of communication between their peoples and to employ these means for the purposes of mutual understanding and a truer and more perfect knowledge of each other's lives;

In CONSEQUENCE WHEREOF they do hereby create the United Nations Educational, Scientific and Cultural Organization for the purpose of advancing, through the educational and scientific and cultural relations of the peoples of the world, the objectives of international peace and of the common welfare of mankind for which the United Nations Organization was established and which its charter proclaims.

81

continuous give and take with others different in nature, distant in space, and remote in time, alike at home and abroad. Arts and letters, like science, spontaneously orchestrate to one another so that no sooner does a land mature a variant in its culture than it is imported by other lands, for the most part without passport and without tariff.

On the record, then, free trade in the things of the spirit is the life of the spirit. Its economy can be an economy of abundance only as its trade is free, at home and abroad. Nothing in such trading can be rigid, fixed, or compulsive. The associations which it develops are mobile themselves and facilitate and protect the mobility of their members: they compose an *open* society, where free communication between all interests constitutes the bond of union between the various communicants. In the sciences and the arts and the letters, yellow men, black men, brown men, and red play on the teams on equal terms with white; Germans, Spaniards, Italians, and Russians exchange their discoveries and creations on equal terms with Frenchmen, Englishmen, Americans, Palestinians, Chinese, and Hindustani. Every local or national culture has an international cultivation. Their ways and works compose a federal union, not a centralized unity. This union is a self-patterning process, wherein an ever-changing One takes form as the orchestration of an ever-changing Many. Its device is truly *e pluribus unum*. The mind which realizes its actualities in their concreteness and chooses its method and matter to be its conscious purpose becomes effectively an international mind.

But if international minds are integral to the being of the arts and sciences, or may be compelled or cultivated by the exigencies of politics and business, such minds are remote from the daily routines of the world's multitudes, panting hopelessly to earn their bread in freedom and to eat it in peace. In the last analysis the problem is: How can an American hillbilly or a Chinese coolie or a Russian peasant or a Hindu untouchable be led to think internationally like a scientist or writer or artist? What price international mind for the great majority, most of whom cannot yet even read or write or reckon?

The obvious answer is: by education, by education with the spoken word, the picture, the word written or printed. Wherever men walk or work or play—in the homes, in the shops, on the fields, in the schools—let the radio speak to them, the motion picture show them, the teacher teach them. But there's the rub. So far neither the ancient nor the modern methods of education; not religion, not ethics, not social science, nor any other discipline has been able to develop in the peoples the habits of feeling, of thinking, and of doing which would make up an international mind. Cults and schools the most sincere and dedicated have produced only habits of talking a union of nations, not ways of living internationally.

To be sustained and to grow, such ways, obviously, would require a lasting ideo-motor set of the personality, a foundation of readiness, with its dynamic of emotion and will. The stimuli which could turn readiness into act would need be any and every item of the daily life that can symbolize to experience a society not one's own. Seeing them, hearing them, tasting them, handling them or using them, should bring to mind as clearly and distinctly as may be the image of people in that society, people effectually related to those items. The feeling that suffuses the total perception would need to be like the feeling that suffuses, among their devotees, perception of the cross, the swastika, the hammer and sickle, the national flag, or the national hero. That is, it would need carry intimations of benefits received and given, returns impelled, and expectancy of more to come; it would need to stir a sense of respect, reassurance, and enlargement. The mood should have an aura alike of dependence and of support.

Take such a commonplace thing as rubber boots. That any American may wear a pair requires a succession of labors by peasants, sailors, railroaders, rubber workers, salespeople, and others of all sorts of origins and cultures. Without the order of their labors the boots cannot come to their ultimate consumer. Suppose that when this one sees them or handles them or wears them, there comes to his mind—at first consciously and then reflexly—the network of human relations of which his rubbers are a node. Suppose that the sense of the peasants and workers and traders to whom he owes his boots has become strongly pleasurable. Then other emotions antagonistic to the idea of the outsider—let the word *xenophobia* suffice for them all—will have that much more resistance to overcome. Attitude will be re-enforced by ideas and may pass over into habit, like the habits which enchannel the relations of children to parents.

Can the schools of any land—to say nothing of the world—so deal with their charges as to set up an international mind? The creation of the United Nations Scientific, Educational and Cultural Organization is testimony to the faith of already internationally minded men and women everywhere in the world that the schools can. Although, however, they function as independent variables, the schools possess neither the inner force nor the autonomy that alone can make them more than sympathetic accessories to the institutional powers which actualize conflict without violence and co-operation without repression; which, in the relation of states and peoples and individuals, enchannel the free conduct of world business in a world of free men.

84

Nevertheless, education is the first resort as well as the last, for a world-wide solution of the problem of freedom. Many fear that all devices are from the first too late, that because of the atom bomb modern man is *obsolete,* and that he will either alter or perish.[22] Such fear is folly.

*   *   *

If the freedom we are born with is impotent, if all men are born equal only in that they are equally helpless and would perish equally without the care and nurture of the elders, this imperceptible spring nevertheless does mount in an ever-mightier *élan,* as work dismantles or warfare breaks through the walls that shut it in; as it seeks, and soon or late wins, the knowledge and the skills which make the free man ever more the captain of his soul and the master of his fate. Modern man *is* modern in that knowledge, through those skills, and his modernity *is* his liberty. Should destruction come, and the world of man return by the hand of man to the subatomic dust whence it freely rose and where it hardily struggled to live and grow, the guilt will not be modern man's. The guilt will fall upon his contemporary who, fearing freedom, fearing open society and the free trade which makes abundance in thoughts and things, demanded of the unlike they should submit their difference and make themselves like to him or else be shut out and beaten down to disaster.

For modern man to prefer safety to freedom is to betray his modernity. For modern man, to be alive is to labor to make the works and ways of all men everywhere the home of freedom—that mankind will defend for freedom's sake. Let us not then fear the battle, if the foes of freedom will the battle. Whenever and however it comes, the free man's readiness is all.

---

[22] See Norman Cousins, *Modern Man Is Obsolete* (New York, 1945).

85

But if we build the free world bravely and without illusion, then, even though we may not make it One World, that battle need never come. The orchestration of mankind goes on. The new scores have been written; the performance is already under way. Let us play the free man's part in the modern organization of freedom. That which Pericles said to the Athenians mourning their dead fallen in battle with totalitarian Sparta, I make bold to repeat to you again, now two thousand years and more thereafter: Let us be about freedom's business, "knowing the secret of happiness to be freedom and the secret of freedom a brave heart."

The Two Anarchisms

AN ADDRESS IN MEMORY OF NICOLA
SACCO AND BARTOLOMEO VANZETTI [1]

MY dear friends. In a certain sense it is improper that I should be at any public meeting this week. I am here by accident and unwillingly. I came to Boston to attend my mother's funeral, but when the committee which has organized this meeting asked me to add my word to that of the others who are speaking here tonight I felt that I had not the right to say no.

Today is exactly a twelvemonth since the seven years of torture of these two innocent men came to a violent end by a modern auto-da-fé. They are at peace. They are beyond the vindictiveness and the malice of a prosecuting attorney who could suppress evidence in order to prevail against their weakness; they are beyond the malice of a vulgar and a prejudiced judge who could venture to sit on his own impartiality. They are beyond the class prejudice and the malice of distinguished justices and university presidents who have made the name of education a byword wherever honest educated men come together. They are beyond the mercilessness and the vindictiveness of a chief executive who has failed to rise to higher political office

---

[1] An address delivered in Boston, Mass., Aug. 23, 1928, and the basis of a warrant for the arrest of the speaker on the charge of blasphemy. The warrant was withdrawn by the authorities before the speaker could return to Boston to accept service.

The address was made extempore. The stenographic record has been somewhat revised for publication.

over their dead bodies. Sacco and Vanzetti are at peace. They deserve their peace. Even the shameful death that was inflicted on them was much easier to accept than were the preceding seven years' torture to bear.

Sacco and Vanzetti were not killed because they were certainly guilty of a crime. The doubt was too great and too widespread among all classes, among experts in all fields. They were killed, first, because they were men of another race and another speech and, secondly, because they were men who dared to think for themselves about political and social problems instead of accepting the conventional lies for which Mr. Fuller and Mr. Thayer and Mr. Lowell receive their unearned increment. They had won to a vision and a faith of their own, and on their own; and their conscience clung to its integrity heedless of the cost to their persons and fortunes. Who can say, beyond doubt, that their faith was true or false? That which they believed may have been delusion and error. I think myself that it was delusion and error. But they had a right to think it, they had a right to teach it; they had a right because what they thought and what they taught they thought and taught out of a great love for mankind.

They were anarchists. Well and good. But there are two kinds of anarchists. One kind is simply a religious sect. One kind holds to a certain gospel about human nature and the structure of society. One kind is an anarchy envisioned out of the love of man. If Sacco and Vanzetti were anarchists, Jesus Christ was an anarchist. If Sacco and Vanzetti were anarchists, Francis of Assisi was an anarchist, Giordano Bruno was an anarchist, Thomas Jefferson was an anarchist, Abraham Lincoln was an anarchist.

There is another kind of anarchy which never is called by its true name. It is not religious but criminal. The practitioner of this kind of anarchy does not recognize himself as an anarchist; he calls himself the champion of law and order. And he is the champion of law and order. But he champions his law and order that he may use them for the purpose of attaining selfish ends, of expropriating the community, of exploiting his fellowmen, of debauching the government and defeating justice, of making the record which is the shame of the United States during the last seven years.

The forces which did Sacco and Vanzetti to death were such champions of law and order, manipulating them, perverting them. They were criminal anarchists. They represent, they have represented from the beginning of our history, those vindictive passions of fear, of greed, and of corruption that have always endeavored to abort, to debase, the ideals of our Republic, that have rendered the Declaration of Independence a byword and put the Bill of Rights to shame. They are the powers of darkness against whom that eternal vigilance which is the price of liberty must always be maintained.

And it is for that reason that the "good shoemaker" and the "poor fishpeddler" must not be forgotten. In themselves they are nothing. Human lives are lost by hundreds of thousands in the United States every year merely as an incident of the normal conduct of industry. In the mere business of making their livings, men find their deaths, and much more numerously than on the battlefields. A life more or less makes little difference. But an ideal more or less, the integrity of the American spirit, that makes all the difference.

We in America especially cannot live by bread alone precisely because we have too much bread, and too much bread kills the spirit. Sacco and Vanzetti, denying themselves bread, clinging to the truth as they had learned to see the truth, have become symbols of that spirit of Amer-

89

ican freedom which we talk about but hardly ever meet any more. Because they are symbols, because their significance has been made by American lovers of American idealism the same as the significance of an American ideal, of the ideal of equal justice and freedom and mercy to all men, we must remember Sacco and Vanzetti. We must remember them lest we forget freedom and justice and mercy.

Wherever Sacco and Vanzetti will be remembered, there freedom and justice and mercy cannot be forgotten. They, in their anarchism of loving-kindness, are symbols of these enduring principles of human fellowship against which the criminal anarchy of vindictive privilege as everlastingly deploys "law," embattles "order," and commands murder. In life, Sacco and Vanzetti were sacrificial victims to this anarchy. But their slaughter at its hands lifts the victims into victory. Wherever the great tradition of American idealism is revered, they will be remembered and reverenced as its symbols. And where they are remembered, neither will the fearful obloquy of the men who sent them to their death be forgotten. Already those men have begun to serve their immortality of shame.

The Warfare of
Religion Against Science

I

IN NEW YORK CITY there stands a new Protestant
church distinguished for novelties. Of those, not the
greatest perhaps, but certainly the most striking is the
election of Ralph Waldo Emerson and Albert Einstein to
the Protestant communion of saints whose stone images
spread an adorning sanctity upon the church's face. Among
the pious the addition of these men's images to the holy
company seemed a sacrilege; to the complacent orthodox,
a grave impropriety; and to the irritable orthodox, a gross
impertinence; whereas to unbelievers it was provocation.
Thus the event became a nine days' scandal among all
classes of the religious community, and the *intelligentsia*
did not miss adding it to the pabulum of their feasts of
reason and flows of soul.

Winning such varied attention, Einstein-among-the-
saints could not fail to receive also editorial notice in the
public prints. Many an oracle was delivered upon the per-
sistently vexatious question of the relations between religion and science, by the anonymous inspired ones whose
editorial deliverances are said to utter and to guide public
opinion. Among the columns and columns it was my
pleasure to review, one, in a liberal metropolitan journal,
seemed to me pat to the habit of mind of liberals of all
classes. This editorial recited a doxology to tolerance and to
the charity of the Christian spirit toward sinners and un-

believers, but it praised tolerance the most. "It is surely worth while," said the oracle, "to try to reconcile religion and science if possible, and such gestures as are implied in the carvings on the façade of the Riverside Church are friendly gestures better calculated to cause men to reason together than would be a gesture of hostility or exclusion. We have long since passed the time when science and religion fought with fagots. This is an age of reason and conciliation."

Some of the assumptions—of fact and ideal—which underlie this statement are characteristic, alike of the liberal and conciliating and modernist members of the community, of the intransigent orthodox, and of the great mass who give the matter no thought at all. They are components of our current common sense, parts of the funded mentality of the man on the street. The assumptions I refer to are that it is science which is waging a war against religion, and that science makes use of the same engines of warfare as religion—"fights with fagots." Even in the richly stored mind of so meticulous and devout a historian of the relationship as Andrew D. White the notion that science is the aggressor is an unconscious postulate, so that he spontaneously entitled his classic review of the action *The Warfare of Science with Theology.* Even the positivistic John Draper speaks without thinking of *The Conflict between Science and Religion.* Science attacks, religion only defends itself; so runs the legend.

On the record, however, this postulate of general opinion turns the facts topsy-turvy. Science is a good dog which has been given a bad name. Says White:

In all modern history interference with science in the supposed interest of religion, no matter how conscientious such interference may have been, has resulted in the direst evils both to religion and to science, and invariably; and, on the other hand,

an untrammelled scientific investigation, no matter how dangerous to religion some of its stages may have seemed for the time
to be, has invariably resulted in the highest good both of religion
and of science.

It is religion that attacks, not science. Unless the mere
existence of science be an attack upon religion, science not
only does not attack religion, it does not defend itself
against religious aggression. With the exception of a few
isolated scientists who, like Huxley, allowed themselves to
be drawn into defensive controversy with ecclesiastics and
theologizing laymen, the history of science and scientists
is a history of complete pacifism and nonresistance toward
religion. Nay, more, it records much friendliness and co-
operation; when scientists do actively consider religion,
they do so to bring it aid and comfort, to sustain and to
strengthen it. During the whole rich history of science in
the western world, from Roger Bacon (a priest of the
Roman Catholic Church whom his spiritual leaders duped
and persecuted) to Millikan the Presbyterian physicist
and Eddington the Quaker astronomer, this has been the
case. It is true, of course, that there are to be found one or
two communions of established religion which acknowledge and welcome the friendly hand. But for every one
such there are scores that regard it with anger and fear.
For the sustenance which is drawn for religion from the
sciences transforms religion, and makes the old god to
wear an unfamiliar face. The Jehovah of Calvin is not the
providence of Millikan, nor is the Heavenly Father of
George Fox identical with the ineffable divinity to which
the consciousness of Arthur Eddington testifies. The institutional religious mind—and in religion the common mind
is institutional—regards science at its most inert as "upsetting," at its friendliest as "destructive," a salvation which
kills.

93

II

Significantly, we find established religion from its earliest beginnings engaged without remission in two wars. One is a civil war against heretics and sectarians. The other is a foreign war against science.

The war against heretics is defensive. A heresy is a challenge to established convention or creed. "The medieval definition of a heretic," says Sumner in his *Folkways*, "is one who varies in life and conversation, dress, speech or manner (that is, social ritual), from the ordinary members of the Christian community." The sentiment underlying this definition continues to prevail. A heresy is regarded as being by intention a denier, an enemy, and a pretender. The orthodox believe that its whole being is concentrated upon pulling down their Old Truth, if it can, and setting up its own infallibility in the place thereof. Heresies arise in two ways: by faction and fission within the boundaries of established religion itself, or by natural impregnation from without. During the past century and a half, science has been perhaps the richest external source of heretical fecundation. For example, the encyclical *Pascendi Dominici Gregis* which Pius IX promulgated in 1907, was preceded by a "Syllabus of Modern Heresies" prescribed by a decree (*Lamentabili sane Exitu*) of the Holy Roman and Universal Inquisition. The substance of each, the decree and the encyclical, consists of an enumeration of the changes generated in the views of Catholic conscientious scholars by contact with the data of the sciences, particularly the biological and social sciences. (The purpose of both is to anathematize these changes, to forbid all study and consideration of them, and to lay such persons as do consider or hold them under the ban.) Again, Protestant Modernism, so perennially awakening the righteous anger of the fundamentalists, is simply Protestant doctrine inwardly altered because of the assimilation of data, opinions, and teachings taken by devout Protestant religionists from the sciences.

In these takings and mutations and their consequences among religious establishments, science has no intentional share whatsoever, any more than a spring has when boys drink of its waters. The sciences are simply at hand, simply present in the landscape of religious life as the wind and the rain are present, or the stones and the seeds of the earth. Their activities do not involve God or sin or salvation or immortality whether as materials, as tools, or as ends; their duties and labors are not occupied with them. The business of the sciences is wholly with their subject matter, whether it be the stars of the heaven, the stones of the earth, the birds of the air, the fish of the sea, or whatever else may be found above, beneath, or between. These the men of science observe and examine and manipulate, seeking to decide what they are made of, how they are put together, how they move and act alone and in companies, and what results therefrom. To accomplish these ends the sciences have prepared tools and techniques which they are ever concerned to improve and perfect. So they render the knowledge they gain ever more precise and ever more available to the uses of mankind. This is their business. They are absorbed in it and mind no other. They are not concerned to guard or promote what they accomplish. They leave it free and every man may take as he chooses and use as his heart desires.

III

That the religionist finds perforce many things among the works of science to prize and to appropriate is due to the fact that the domain and the function of science and religion among the arts of life coincide, or very nearly do so. Hence religion, the incomparably more venerable of the establishments of civilization, begins by looking upon science, still a mere babe in swaddling clothes, as an upstart and an interloper. This attitude, spontaneous enough in the days of Galileo and Descartes, has now become a fixed habit stronger than original nature. It is unconditional in religion, an inborn movement of its proper life, not a response brought forth by an inimical regard which science turns upon it. The fact is that the regard of science is not upon religion at all. The regard of science is upon science. Science has never sized up religion as a prize fighter sizes up his opponent in the prize ring. But religion has always sized up science as a prize fighter sizes up his opponent in the prize ring, searching, searching for weak points and errors, and seeking ever to beat science down if not to knock it out.

The reason is that religion sees science doing its own work in its own field better than it can itself.

For what is religion, and what does religion do? Definitions are legion. Most, however, are really redefinitions brought into existence by the pressure of variations in the social environment—economic, political, and aesthetic as well as scientific—upon the religious establishment, and imposing constant shifts of its vital balance to keep it from getting completely upset. Beneath all the variety and contradiction in definition there flows nevertheless a single continuous sentiment and a single continuous purpose and a single repetitive pattern of behavior. These continuities and repetitions impart to the most contradictory definitions a certain consistency and intelligibility, as the drives in a man's character impart to the disorder and obscurity of his single acts a natural clear unity. Thus it may be said that all definitions, from the most fundamentalist to the most modernist, are agreed that the function of religion is to save what men hold most dear, to save from day to day and for eternity. And what religion *does,* generates and establishes what religion is.

Now, as Job declares, there appears to be a warfare to man upon earth; he is born unto trouble as the sparks fly upward. However it may have been in the beginning, the world which mankind have inhabited since before religion took place among them does not behave as if it was made for them, all serenity and beneficence and security. Their life persists in being mostly hazard and struggle, hardship and fear—an effort beset by dangers and terminating in death. To overcome the dangers and to vanquish death have ever been the declared tasks of the religious enterprise. Religion figures as a heroic instrument in the human struggle to survive, a device with which to gain and to hold beyond any peradventure food, clothing, shelter, mastery over enemies and disease, the succession of the generations in this life, and the nullification of death for "the life eternal." These ends religion accomplishes by force of an account of the origin and character of the world and of man and a use of this account. Religion consists of a sacred deliverance concerning man's present state and future destiny, and an art of facilitating or averting this destiny by means of highly elaborated special instruments of control, adjustment, and transformation that should destroy evil and further good.

Thus, all religions declare that the world of the daily life is somehow not primary but secondary, somehow a world of falsehood and illusion. Behind or beneath it, they say, throbs an incommensurable real world which is the creator and the ruler of the apparent one. In this real world are concentrated all power and all good. Its stuff is spirit; it is friendly to man and it guarantees that what men hold most precious shall survive forever, victorious over every falsehood and all disaster. There are special tools and techniques which have the potency to obtain effective manifestations of the Cosmic Friendliness. These are uniquely the properties and organs of religion—its sacred images and agents, its relics, its holy places, its revelations, its rituals, its liturgies, its mortifications, its sacraments, and all the other devices used in worship, sacrifice, prayer, and the like.

IV

To a great extent the function and implements of science correspond with the function and implements of religion. Like religion, science regards the world of the daily life as appearance, not reality—appearance only, however, not illusion. Like religion, science declares that an unseen world operates behind the visible one, a world of causes, of power, of efficacy, which generates the apparent world of our experience and which the latter expresses and signifies. Like religion, science invents and perfects devices to uncover, to manipulate, and to control the unseen powers. These are the equipment of the laboratories, the observatories, the industrial plants, with their microscopes and telescopes, their clocks and rules, their furnaces and presses, their mathematical formulae, their texts, and so on.

Neither science nor religion observes its unseen world. Both merely assert that it exists. Electrons, atoms, cosmic rays, and other ultimates postulated by science are no more contents of direct experience than the gods and angels and devils affirmed by religion. No scientist has ever encountered an electron and no believer has ever seen his God. Both draw inferences from events in the world of appearance, treating these events as signs of the hidden power behind.

But the sign as religion uses it is arbitrary, a sign by fiat, therefore illusion. There exists neither a dynamic nor a logical connection between appearance and the reality; the relation is purely allegorical, and any other parable (as the religious philosophers of antiquity, by acknowledging the parity and interchangeability of the cults, well realized) would have done as well. In the language of the theologian this would mean that the creator is utterly independent of his creature, and any other of the infinite possible worlds he chose to create would express his will and purpose as aptly as this one. The world he has produced is a contingent world, a fabrication, a tale that is told, not a growth that develops; and the teller is, like Mr. Whitehead's "principle of concretion," himself in no way involved in the events he tells of.

For science, per contra, appearance is the appearance of reality. The connection between the two is both dynamic and logical, so that the appearance is by nature at once an expression and a sign of the reality. Ordinary experience taken piecemeal or as a whole, in which the scientific enterprise starts, is naturally also what it ends in. The case is different with religion. Religions ascribe their knowledge of the unseen world to some ineffable unique translumination which is called mysticism when interpreted liberally, and revelation when the interpretation is orthodox. This translumination is not sharable, yet it is infallible and overruling. The knowledge, the power, and the privilege which it brings cannot be transmitted as experience, but only as recollection and tradition. Their validity hence is a matter of faith alone. It lies beyond proof, residing in authority only. God the Father tells Jesus, Jesus tells Peter and the Apostles, and they commit the deposit of faith to their successors, each in his generation. So, in the Christian world, the Church and its authority are established, vindicated, and sustained—by an aboriginal revelation which recurs once or twice or thrice, to Noah, to Abraham, to Moses, to Jesus, and then stops, and its secret is carried by authority and tradition from one generation of power to another.

And so with all revealed religions. The revelation is declared to be unique, universal, eternal, immutable, and its guardian infallible. Any and every divergence from it thus becomes *ipso facto* falsehood, faction, sin, and its supporter a heretic whose wages is justly death. Since many divergences and variations automatically happen and some survive, established religion comes to embody a congeries of mutually contradictory and opposed dogmas. The champions of each necessarily proclaim theirs as the sole universal, eternal, and exclusive truth, the only way to life everlasting, and denounce the alternatives and competitors as compounds of falsehood leading to death. The entire history of religion is thus a record of inner conflicts and diversifications, of sects multiplying geometrically and surviving arithmetically. Comparatively few of the numbers and varieties that are born attain the organization and property which enable them to persist. In the salad days of Christianism extermination of the variants at the hands of their more powerful rivals was a foregone conclusion. And always the potential anarchy among those that survive is kept amenable to law and order by the interplay of the other institutions of civilized life.

V

Such a mutual confrontation of exclusive infallibilities could not help being a deep, unacknowledged factor in the claim which religions make to priority in the task of educating the young. The claim has its historic grounds too. When Christianity first appeared as a power strong enough to get attention, education was a voluntary enterprise in the hands of great secular schools such as those in Athens, Pergamos, Alexandria. The Christians were hard put to it to defend their revelation of nature and destiny against the criticism of pagan philosophers and scholars. Such of the early Christian literature as is not liturgical is either polemic or apology; "apologetics" is still a discipline of theological seminaries. It was not merely because the schools were teaching error that the priesthood had them shut up when Christianism came to power as the religion of the state; it is because shutting them relieved it of too heavy an intellectual burden. Dealing with heresies was bad enough; when it came to the arguments and ridicule of reasonable pagan men of culture, it was too much; these must be stopped at the source. Thus the closing of the schools endowed the Christian doctors with a double prerogative; it eliminated a materially weak but emotionally demoralizing opposition and it made of education a monopoly of the church.

The Protestant Reformation changed the monopoly from a single and general ecclesiastical control to a plural and local one. It initiated also a great multiplication of sects, and those which survived were so approximately equal in power that the state could not with safety favor any. Its role changed. Whereas it used to be the "secular arm" of one ruling church, it now was an impartial guardian of the liberties of many churches, none of which was strong enough to venture to rule. Church and state were "separated" and presumably remain so. The effect of this separation upon education, when education became a matter of public interest, was inevitably to separate that also from religion and to shift the weight of the civil power toward secularism.

This, naturally, aggravates the ecclesiastical claim. No sect fails to beat at the door of the school, weekdays and Sabbath, deploring the corruption and moral decay which, ecclesiastics declare, follow the withdrawal of "religious education." Only because the sects are many and their doctrines varied and their jealousies burning is this education not a part of the national curriculum. Although only the Catholics present the claim as insuperable, its logic is identical for all the sects. It still finds its due conclusion in the Catholic pretension that the right to teach belongs exclusively to the Church, that nothing can be taught contrary to the established faith, and that schools for the children of the faithful must receive the sanction of ecclesiastical authority (on occasion sacraments have been refused to parents whose children attend schools uncertified by such authority). "As a mandate to teach," asserts the current Pope in his recent encyclical on education, "Christ conferred infallibility in educative work on his church." And the rest follows.

However this assertion may satisfy true believers, unbelievers, who are now very numerous and powerful, require reasons, and to them it is declared that the young souls must be strengthened against the temptations of sin and error by which they are beset from birth and that indoctrination in the sole truth, of which the church is the sole guardian, and discipline in right habits of obedience to the divinely constituted authority of the guardian are alone the strengtheners. From this doctrine and discipline ensue virtue, character, and salvation. What price alternatives, then? What price tolerance? Don't tell your children about tolerance, a clerical spokesman admonishes 1,200 members of a chapter of the Catholic Teachers' Association, but inspire them with enthusiasm for their church. . . . The Catholics have the license of their numbers and of the age and the power of their ecclesiastical establishment. Other cults would say as much for themselves if they dared.

Whatever the heavenly outcome of excluding the young from the study and judgment of alternatives, religious or secular, its effect in the workaday world is to turn education into a spiritual sausage machine which macerates and molds the endless variety of the things that go into the hopper, into the identical shape, size, and material of the things that come out. It imposes a mental and moral conformity whose universal effect is to make of each new generation a means merely for the upkeep of the particular ecclesiastical establishment. Men, it implies, were made for the Church, not the Church for men. By contrast, the influence of science upon education has been to generate an attitude of respect for the original nature and developing personality of the human young, and to shift the educative process from the techniques of indoctrination and discipline to techniques of inquiry, experimentation, and discovery. Because of science, the consensus spreads that education must be a tool not to reproduce an ancient pattern but to help each crescent psyche to grow into its own appropriate maturity and freedom.

VI

That the pioneers into the religious unknown, the modernists and others at the frontiers of religion, do not share the prevalent ecclesiastical attitude toward education does not mitigate the prevalence. Devout spirits who have more than once been shocked by the attitude have challenged it, without in any way modifying its trends. Emerson had had his forerunners as he has been

103

having his successors when he advised young candidates for the ministry to "cast conformity behind you and acquaint men at first hand with the deity." But the very nature of a first-hand acquaintance with the deity precludes that it shall be an experience even of few, to say nothing of the multitudes. The millions are permitted no acquaintance with the deity except at second hand a thousand times removed. They confront it never in direct vision, but ever through the mediating glass of tradition, authority, priestcraft.

The unseen world of the sciences, on the contrary, calls for no mediation, no intercession. Anyone who will take the trouble may reach it as directly as the specialist himself. In fact, no kind of acquaintance with scientific data, direct or indirect, may be held as valid unless it has been participated in by many men, even the multitudes. Where religion takes its ground on revelation, science appeals to experience; where religion imposes authority and tradition, science invites free experimentation and testing; where religions assert the primacy and eternity of their respective revelations, to the exclusion of all alternatives, science acknowledges the genuineness and validity of the alternatives, the reality of change, and keeps perfecting a technique for the progressive and fair testing of all alternatives. Religion, in sum, imposes a grammar of assent, while science invites participation in a logic of doubt and inquiry.

The result is a paradox. Religion, starting with a single universal infallible revelation to be imposed without exception on all men, comes out with a clashing multitude of such revelations, eternally at war with one another, since each claims to be the unique truth and only one can be. Science, starting with a multitude of alternatives, each with a claim to validity, ends up with a consensus that one of these claims has made itself good. The religious revelation glorifying its single, inviolable universality and eternity makes for an ever greater particularity, variety, and multiplicity. The scientific theories, starting in multiplicity and variety of observation, tend toward an ever completer harmonization and generality, until they emerge in a unified and universal system owning the free assent of all concerned in the initial differences.

This consummation follows from the fact that science practices spiritual modesty and intellectual economy, minding ever its own business only. The answer which Laplace gave Napoleon points the contrast between it and religion. "What place have you in this theory for God?" the emperor asked after he had heard the great astronomer explain his nebular hypothesis of the origin of heavenly bodies. "Sire," the legend reports Laplace as saying, "I have no need for that hypothesis." Religionists cannot cease to reprobate this reply. It discommodes even devout modernists to whom it is recalled. Yet it is a beatitude of scientific humility and probity. For Laplace was not concerned either with proving or disproving the existence and power of God. He was concerned only to establish, by means of the fewest and simplest elements possible, a working and fruitful account of the systems of the heavens. He had done so. Adding God would have added no workable efficacy, no measurable power, no law statable as a proportion between quantities of substance. It would have been to multiply causes without occasion, to have violated the so profitable principles of simplicity and parsimony, to have confused the theory without making the facts any more amenable to reason or the will. Laplace did not exclude God from among the possible hypotheses; he only found that he could do better without this hypothesis, that it was not needed. Had he needed it, he would have used it. Religionists, per contra, demand that this hypothesis shall be used, need or no need. They would compel its addition, by any and every means within their reach, to all theories of origins, operations, and outcomes of the universe and all the inhabitants thereof. They would impose it regardless, whether it belong or not, whether it hinder or help. They require that whatever goes on shall, in the words of the Spanish adieu, go with God.

VII

This peculiarity of the religious disposition rests, deep down, upon the profound but generalized vital fear which is our consciousness of the essential imbalance and hazard of organic existence. Nearer the surface, it utters the actual strain between the rival divine infallibilities offered as security against imbalance; and it reflects the glamour of that extreme beneficence and power wherewith the spirit of man had anciently invested the imputed sources of this security. These sources are the gods and the arts by which their support is encompassed on behalf of the hope of man. Where they work, attainment is foreordained. How then shall one endure that they fail anywhere? Millennia before science was born, religion lived, the one instrument of security and salvation in a beset and treacherous world. Its doctrine, its discipline, its technique seemed to be all that stood between man's survival and man's extinction. Conception and birth; puberty, marriage, and death; warfare; herding and tillage; the arts of the potter and the smith; the turn of the stars and the sun; the seasons' round, the renewal and the fruitfulness of the earth; sickness, sorrow, and healing—whence could they be, save from the gods? And how could they hurt or prosper save by the divine intervention secured with due and reverent ritual, meticulously correct? The art

106

of moving the gods could not help becoming the queen of the arts, with all the other arts of life as its mere hand-maidens, as accessories and supernumeraries, not principals. Nothing that men feared could be averted, nothing that they hoped for could be attained, save by means of the techniques of religion. In a very real and pregnant sense religion held a monopoly in solutions for the ever-welling problems of human existence.

And this was the state of things when science appeared upon the scene. At bottom, the moral and operational difference between science and religion derives from the discovery that the arts hitherto esteemed as merely accessory and supernumerary, the handmaiden arts, not only work as well without the superimposed religious techniques but often far better, with an enhanced vitality and efficiency. Science is the liberation of these arts; conversely their stuffs and their ways are the generators of science. As sciences they become, even in the hands of obedient churchmen like Copernicus or Mendel or Bussac or Loisy (most of them are sooner or later disciplined for it or even excommunicated), autonomous bodies of knowledge, principals, masters in their own right. They cease to have need of the religious hypothesis.

It can hardly be without import that none of the pioneers of the new sciences, none of the liberators of the hand-maiden arts, when he began his observations and experiments and speculations, was aware of the implications of his attitude. Not Copernicus, not Tycho Brahe, not Kepler, not Galileo, not Harvey, not Leeuwenhoek, not Newton, not Dalton, not Boyle. Most of them believed they were vindicating afresh and more completely than ever before the ways of God to man. They were innocent of any idea that their labors were tantamount to invading a monopoly rather than re-enforcing it. The men of religion, however,

107

appear from the first to have sensed, even if they did not understand, that such was the case. Their attack on science followed with no delay, and it has been maintained without remission to this day. Statutes in Tennessee about evolution are merely the 1930 descendants of decrees in Rome about Copernicanism.

VIII

Without remission, I say. Without remission in spite of the fact, nay, because of the fact, that the warfare of religion against science has been a losing warfare from its very beginning, with ever-shifting fronts, and since recent years has proceeded in the form of a rear-guard action. For the role of the religious art as the middleman between the other arts of life and their success has faded to practically nothing. Its monopoly is at an end. The godless agriculture of the scientific farmer of America, Western Europe, and Russia proves to be a more successful method of tillage than the devout farming of the Spaniards, Hindus, Arabs, Chinese, and others who "go with God." The scientific breeder outprospers the religious one; meteorology enables a far more adequate meeting of weather conditions than prayer; the art of medicine does so much better for the sick and the well than exorcism and the intercession of saints that even the Pope, when he is ill, adds the best available physician to the help of God. By and large, the men and women of the lands where science has a free hand live more healthily, more comfortably, are better sheltered, fed, clothed, and protected than the men and women of the lands where science does not prevail.

We sum up this eventually by saying that life has become secularized. But how, and why? Certainly not because the sciences have occupied themselves with fighting religion. On the contrary, even in religious settings, they are too busy with their own affairs ever to bother with religion. It is that needy and sorrowful men turn more and more from religion to science for assuagement of their sorrows and satisfaction of their necessities. Religion has been shifting with an increasing momentum from the center of life to its periphery, from a monopoly of all its interests to a recessive claimant upon some of them. This situation is a historic event, a fact to be studied and understood, not a vice or mortal sin to be denounced and exorcised. It exists because of what, at heart, religion is and what, at heart, science is, and not because of a nonexistent assault of science upon religion. It argues no virtue in science nor any turpitude in religion. Each serves, in its own characteristic fashion, the ends of human life. Maybe an ironist in the nature of things leads the event so to fall out that wherever observation and understanding are possible, wherever the living mind has play and room the best of religion is not quite so good as the best of science and the worst of science not quite so bad as the worst of religion. Whence it also falls out that religion is with all reverence permitted to recede into a natural desuetude.

In certain fields, religion has quite given up its labors, though not its pretensions. Such fields are physics, mechanics, and chemistry, their derivatives and the arts based on them.

In others, religion seeks a compromise.

Such a field is biology, in which the devout champion the vitalistic hypothesis or concede, as do Catholics, that evolution accounts for bodies but has no meaning for immortal souls which are newly created with each birth and grow only better or worse, but not different.

Such a field is disease and death. Disease is a realm of poignant uncertainty and insecurity. Medical science, al-

though it has improved health and prolonged life far
beyond what our forebears could hope for, is still a long,
long way from a complete conquest of the pathogenic
enemies of the human race. There are diseases no doctor
can heal; there are untimely deaths no medicine can put
off. Here, then, is a domain which religions may forcefully
dispute. They enter a *caveat* against the power and functions of medical science regarding disease and death. They
hold out to the sick, the dying, the mourners the promise
of divine healing, of eternal life, of earthly consolation. And
how shall the suffering hearts of men fail to be persuaded
by a promise so reassuring? How shall such a promise not
serve as a bulwark against the pangs and hazards of a be-
deviled world? Of the power of this promise we have testimony in the recurrence of such cults with pretensions to
healing as Christian Science. To the power of this promise
that piteous and sardonic scene which was enacted not so
long ago in a Catholic graveyard in Malden, Massachusetts
is witness. There, through long weeks, by day and by night,
in fair weather and foul, gathered crowding multitudes of
men, women, and children, sick with every manner of disease, in their hands bearing gifts and votive candles, in their
hearts starving to touch the grave of an obscure priest dead
a hundred years, because they had heard that its touch
gives healing. Those sick ones were not Catholics only, or
unknown, or lowly, or poor. They came from every faith,
from every class, and every rank and station—Jews were
among them, and Mohammedans, Protestants of every
sect, officials and workingmen, nobodies and notorieties,
criminals, policemen, rich people with great presents, poor
ones anxious because their gifts were so small. Also infidels
came.—And so it is with every new shrine of healing and
every new healing cult: the kindly light leads on.

And so it is with the nullification of death, with immortality. Science can sometimes resuscitate; it is forever help-less to resurrect. When death at last has happened, despite all the ardent striving to prevent it, the event is acknowl-edged with due regret and reverence for the dead, and the labor of living goes its way as must needs be. Science can hardly be said to concern itself with immortality, with the denial of death. In this occupation religion remains alone, its monopoly unbroken. When religion, at the graveside, affirms before the stark shape in the coffin, "There is no death," and challenges science to contradict, science only replies, "Not proved." For that assertion of religion's cannot be tested by observation or analysis or experiment through which proof comes, for science; and beyond this testing science has no obligation to regard it. Hence the devout astronomer Millikan says fairly enough: "Concerning what ultimately becomes of the individual, it [evolution] . . . has added nothing and subtracted nothing." Science simply does not deny, when religion asserts, immortality. The churches continue without let or hindrance from science to bring the glad tidings that men are alive when they are dead.

IX

Another domain over which religion claims sole juris-diction is what is commonly known as morality. In its broadest denotation, morality would embrace the entire panorama of human relations—the economic and political establishments, the family, the fine arts, war and peace, everything. And frequently enough religionists endeavor to direct the wrath or the benevolence of heavenly power toward each and all of these matters. (A recent splendid effort of this kind was the solemn Mass intoned by the Pope himself for the purpose of vindicating religion against

111

the imputed aggression of the godless Russian republic. This ritual, whose fame was spread all over the world, made the high point in a mass enterprise, a crusade of prayer against the Russians, by all the Christian sects.)

In the main, however, morality means to religionists the correct ritual of sex behavior, and their oracles on this subject range from comment on the modesty or immodesty of women's clothing to scolding impatient young love, reproving divorce, and denouncing birth control and other applications of intelligence to sex.

Birth control is the liveliest field in the domain of morality, for here science has made observations and drawn conclusions and the religious establishment has drawn up its battalions. Science commends birth control. Its summary of advantages accruing from birth control to human life is clear and definitive. All the modernist and some of the orthodox cults have come unwillingly, but all the more tellingly, to acknowledge its findings. But the more traditional and fundamentalist religious establishments have opposed birth control from of old, and the present law of the land obeys the ancient voice of the church. Historians, economists, biologists, physicians are united on the advisability of teaching the theory and practice of contraception. The consensus is general that many of the most tragic moral issues of history, such issues as war versus peace, individual rights versus social power, freedom versus authority, private property versus commonwealth, arise from the push of populations compressed in territories and vocations too small for their needs. The population problem is acknowledged to be the most fundamental problem of our civilization. Hence the conclusion of the social sciences: conscious control of the growth of population, that is, birth control by scientific means, is essential to the peace and well-being of the masses of mankind. It is common knowledge that unscientific birth control has been at all times openly or secretly but widely practiced among all classes and on all levels of society, from Australian primitives and Periclean Greeks to Spanish sophisticates and American Puritans, and that its consequences are intolerable pain and suffering to women, lives of mutilation and disease, horrible death. In some countries, such as orthodox Russia, abortion had been so prevalent that even the revolutionary Soviet government could not prevent the practice and had to content itself with regulation and sanitary medical control, thus preventing much suffering and the loss of many women's lives.

Yet the great religious establishments of at least the western world are inexorably set against birth control. Whatever its tested advantages to mankind, it shall not be practiced since it violates the revealed law of God. And with not insignificant irony, the clergy who are loudest in damning birth control as an evil are the priests of the Roman Catholic Church. By the decision of the Council of Trent, still operative as ever, it is a doctrine of this church that virginity or celibacy is better, is more blessed, than marriage, and to be preferred; those who deny it are accursed. It is a view general among the orthodox, deriving from St. Paul, that the pangs of childbirth are woman's expiation of Eve's sin in eating the fruit of the tree of knowledge of good and evil. From this the step is simple to the conclusion that using anaesthetics to ease the pangs of childbirth defeats God's justice and is to be avoided. On whatever grounds, the professional religionists of the Catholic Church are vowed to keep themselves in the state of virginity or celibacy, which are the extreme means of birth control. Those who succeed in maintaining this state are necessarily innocent of all knowledge of the realities of the sex function. Those who do not must acquire such knowledge illicitly by breaking their vows and thus are compelled to practice birth control to cover up their sin. So great is the ecclesiastical anxiety over this subject that in communities where the craft has power it may not even be publicly discussed. This is the situation in most of the communities of the United States.

The desuetude into which religion is passing, it is clear, still needs to go far to reach the innocuous. But it is on the way, and knows it is on the way, as the clamor of its claims attests. These become more insistent with the gathering momentum and scope of its recession. Naturally. From the beginning possessor of political, social, and economic privilege, how could religion fail to fight with all its power to maintain its crumbling dignities and station? It demands— and receives—from the state, from the school, from the whole cultural complex of the common life aid and comfort in the enforcement of its prescriptions and taboos— from Sabbath observance to contraception—and other favoring handicaps. Those who are unable to esteem its character or to believe in its divinities are reviled as somehow unfit for the fellowship of mankind. In earlier days they were adjudged criminals worthy of death and so treated; today, since they are too numerous, since secularization has gone too far, the outcry against them is "moral." "Materialism, degradation!" religion proclaims against the spirit of science and the manifest benefactions of its works and ways. And to the generations grown heedless of its warnings and prospectuses, religion cries "Repent, repent! How dare you go on living without that without which you cannot live! You owe religion a debt greater than to anything else in in the world. Pay or perish!" And the state, the school, and the economic establishment are pressed to coerce the generations into payment.

Manifestly, this clamor, this insistence on privilege and demand for more, is not the sign of a power self-assured and unafraid. Modernists in religion know this well and are distressed by the contrast to the quiet self-possession with which science goes about its business. As the spiritual leader of the church among whose stone images Einstein is canonized, observed:

Nobody solicitously is trying to save science for the simple reason that in its own sphere science is saving us. . . . Science is not yet an organization to be maintained or a final creed to be preserved; it is still in the creative vigor of individual venturesomeness and exploitation. . . . Turn however to religion! . . . Multitudes of people are out with props trying to shore up religion . . . until the impression prevails that the major business of churchmen is to keep religion going.

The multitudes bringing "props" bring them from every domain of human thought and action. But especially are they ardent to bring them from science itself. There is a new type of theologian who is all eloquence about the glories of scientific method in religion, the uses of experimentation and the like, until one might think that religion had come to terms with science and become a laborer in its vineyard following its ways. But such is not the case. The "props" which are used to shore religion up, even when borrowed from science, are used willy-nilly with the purpose at the same time to break science down.[1]

Apparently, with the best intentions, religion cannot help waging a warfare against science. And its assaults at all times and under all circumstances make the impression of being not only aggressive battle upon a nonresistent neighbor, but an unfair and an uncivilized battle.

---

[1] See, for example, two books regarded with approval by pious modernists, *Religious Experience and Scientific Method* and *The Wrestle of Religion with Truth*, especially the latter. The author is Henry Nelson Wieman, a professor of theology in the University of Chicago.

X

That religion should find itself impelled to anger by the presence of science and committing acts of violence against it is not difficult to understand. Even the religious establishment, whatever it may claim to the contrary, has arisen in a world which was not made for it, and in which it must struggle and change if it desires to survive. In the order of nature any alternative to religion is a competitor of religion, and existence, on all its levels, enacts only one drama—the drama of the competitive life. Competition rules in nature at least not less than in human affairs, though theology has views suggesting the contrary. If human affairs improve upon nature in this respect, they do so by exacerbation and iniquity. They add something to nature which was not there before. The struggle for survival is in nature a comedy; in civilization it is a tragedy, made so through additions brought—unwittingly enough—by the spirit of man. For within kinds and species, the competitors are never directed toward each other, but toward the attainment of a common end. Differences between success and failure are due to differences in the performance of a function; they are not differences in force or size but differences in perfection. Trees in a wood, growing toward the air and the light, are not in the human sense struggling with each other at all; yet for each one that survives, many perish. That they perish is not the consequence of a hurt they have received from the survivor; it is the consequence of their inability to keep pace with his growth toward the light. When animals flee from the enemies which prey on them, those that are caught may be said to have been in competition with those that escape. But the victims are such through no deed of their peers against them; it is their own slowness which has made them victims, not the speed of the saved.

Men observe this phenomenon in nature and revere its principle. There is in every language a term which appreciates it. In English the term is *sportsmanship* or *fair play*. Sometimes the doubtful term *honor* figures as an equivalent. That sportsmanship has come to signify more in the games of the race than in its business writes its own commentary on life's enterprises and on the compulsions they work upon the soul of man. Whatever the race men run, sportsmanship assures that it shall truly be to the swift. It requires that men shall start without advantage, proceed without privilege, and win by superior strength and skill alone. It bans improper force in the strong against the weak, cunning or fraud in the weak against the strong. It requires a glad acquiescence in the success by which excellence is signalized. It guarantees that only excellence shall be so signalized. The runner may win only by his superiority in the art of running, not by tripping or crowding or threatening his competitors. The same relations are prescribed, if not established, in the practice of all of the peaceful positive arts of civilization, such as medicine, farming, building, needlework, carving, and so on and on. Sportsmanship or fair play requires that the difference between failure and success, survival and extinction, shall be a difference in the completeness wherewith the function in question is performed, a difference between incompetence and mastery. The physician who succeeds as physician and not for other causes is the one who best heals the sick and keeps the healthy in health. The carpenter or plumber or painter, the butcher or baker or candlestick maker who would naturally prosper is he who does the same work better than his competitors. Plato was so impressed with this observation that he saw in it the very essence of justice and wrote the *Republic* to celebrate it.

117

Now in science, justice as sportsmanship is even more conspicuous than in the sports. Competition is the very life of science; everything is done to evoke and encourage it, for indeed, competition and collaboration are there one and the same action. Let a scientist in this field or that make a new observation, propound a new theory, work out a new experiment. Does he keep it a secret? On the contrary, when the competition in his own mind has been won, when he has resolved his own doubts and feels satisfied that he has done everything in his power to avoid error, he proclaims his novelty to the world. Does he then demand unquestioning assent and send apostles upon a mission to induce or impose this assent? Rather, he invites doubt and inquiry, he calls for alternatives, for further research to repeat the observation, to test out the theory, to perform the experiment again, and still again. Soon a collective endeavor becomes manifest whose essence is that each participant seeks to do the same thing better than the others, an endeavor of a type which involves mutual aid as an integral part of attaining competitive success. Scientists not only do not hinder, they help their fellows even while laboring to win over them. There are today in different parts of the world a whole army of men and women absorbed in trying to work out a cure for phthisis. The discoverer of such a cure will be an honored benefactor of mankind. He will certainly gain glory, perhaps wealth. And are not wealth and glory usually motives for exclusiveness, monopoly, secrecy, and a pretension to certainty? But mutually competitive though they be, these scientific researchers are constantly exchanging records and opinions, constantly testing each other's theories, and checking up each other's results. Their competitive aim animates a great co-operative humanitarian enterprise in which the best man, the most skillful and competent, wins over his fellows, and the victory nevertheless belongs to the defeated as well.

Considered in terms of this mode of competition, so general and straight and open in nature, so rare and specialized and distorted among human beings, it is doubtful whether the men who work through religion have brought to mankind such a prospering of the enterprises of civilization, such an enlargement of the good life, as the men who work through sciences. The inventors of fire, the wheel, the lever, the steam engine, and the other devices of industrial civilization have accomplished more which is deserving of the grateful reverence of mankind than the inventors of the gods and the promulgators of religious ways of salvation. In terms of their consequences to the health, the comfort, the security, and the joy of life, the labors of men like Pasteur or Watt or Faraday or Edison or Ford have earned better at the hands of mankind than the labors of men like Jesus or Moses or Buddha or Mohammed.

There exists, I think, throughout the religious establishment a dim sense that this is so and an uneasy fear of what it can lead to. Hence flows another motive for the warfare of religion against science, and for the fact that it is a warfare uncivilized and unfair. If it be true, as all the numbers and varieties of the churches unanimously declare, that religions are dedicated to the present attainment and the eternal possession of the "highest good," the "highest social values," "the enjoyment of God," it is not difficult to understand how such an end might be considered to justify any means. The spirit underlying the logic of the Society of Jesus is no peculiarity of that society or of the Church upon which it spreads glory; this spirit is spontaneous to the ecclesiastical establishment in all of its protean forms. It is the spirit of an institution at bay.

119

XI

For the method of religion is not to excel the competitor by the better performance of an identical task. The method of religion is by force or fraud to eliminate the competitor from the field of endeavor and to keep it a monopoly. Elimination is sometimes accomplished by silencing the competitor, sometimes by imprisoning him, sometimes by driving him out of the community of the saved (excommunication), sometimes by torturing and maiming him, finally by killing him. During the past century and a half, the obviously harsh devices have fallen more and more into public disfavor; the Inquisition no longer feels free to make use of the prison, the torture chamber, the *auto-da-fé* (of books as well as people). But the other methods still obtain, and the subsident ones have been replaced by new forms less likely to stir public disapproval. Especially important are the sly invocation of the mores *via* defamatory whispering campaigns and the bold or subtle uses of social, political, and economic pressure. This stops at no person and no function. One recalls the 1912 assault on the heretical William Howard Taft for being openly and boldly a Unitarian, thus not a Christian; and there must be present in everybody's mind the later attack on Mr. Hoover, who could not make a most commonplace historical summary of the consequences of the Protestant Reformation without being pilloried in the press as violating his oath of office by spokesmen for a sect eager not only to vindicate its own claimed prerogatives but ardent to prevent any gain or glory from accruing to its competitors and alternatives.

As for the classic instrumentalities for eliminating the competitor, the idea is widespread in liberal circles that they have been abandoned. This is however not so; emphasis has been shifted from one kind to another and the occasions of their use are perhaps more carefully studied. The old techniques of the Inquisition have been replaced by milder ones and perhaps altogether limited now to examining and condemning questionable doctrine. But the Censorship is more alive and of wider scope than ever, and the Index Expurgatorius is an indispensable adjunct to the upkeep of the ecclesiastical monopolies. In one way or another, all the sects make use of both these devices. They are universal and endemic to the ecclesiastical process. If opinion regards them as belonging to the Catholics, it is only because the Catholics used them earlier and because this long usage has imparted to them greater finish and preciser ritual form. The Christian Scientists may work them with as thorough an efficiency if not as complete an elegance. The legislative and police power of the state likewise remains a general and important agency for eliminating competition. So, courts may invalidate men's testimony because they are atheists, and legislatures may pass laws compelling Sabbath observance and revamp or enact laws against blasphemy, evolution, and birth control. Indeed any ecclesiastical taboo or prescription may commandeer the secular police power in behalf of its enforcement. Sometimes, when these major devices are not available, bribery is resorted to: the endeavor of the Jewish community of Amsterdam so to silence Spinoza is the classic instance; it failed, and they excommunicated him.

And so the tale tells itself of the effort of religion to eliminate science as a competitor in the field. The use of the devices I have just reviewed figures continuously, from the beginnings in the sufferings imposed upon Roger Bacon to the latest antievolution law. The well-known spirits subjected to suffering or martyrdom for their scientific or dissident faith—Copernicus, Cecco d'Ascoli, Giordano Bruno, Galileo, Castellio, Servetus, Spinoza, Voltaire—are only a handful in the long procession that passes through Andrew White's epic of the warfare of religion against science; and the number of those who have found themselves under the *odium theologicum* since this scholar's time is not small. The record tells of lives threatened, bodies tortured, families disgraced, fortunes confiscated, reputations tarnished, souls outlawed because of a saying of this or of that contrary to the doctrine or policy of a religious establishment. It tells of writings, the most important—or the most unimportant—in the history of science, listed upon one ecclesiastical index or another. Books upon an index are forbidden books. The faithful may not read them. And such reading as is permitted the faithful must be sanctioned by a censor, lest something competitive with the dogmas of the cult come before their minds, and its monopoly over their beliefs be challenged and invaded.

A modern instance points the moral if it does not adorn the tale. Some years ago the Cardinal Archbishop of the Catholic Diocese of Massachusetts caused a slight stir in the public press by denouncing the theory of relativity and its author. The reverend gentleman assigned two reasons for warning his flock against them. The first was that he could not understand relativity. The second was that he was sure it made for atheism. Now the Catholic Church glories in a revelation which embodies several impenetrable mysteries. It insists indeed that such mysteries are a sign of its divine mandate and that this inheres in the fact that such events as the immaculate conception, the virgin birth, the resurrection, the descent into hell, the eucharist (wherein the sacramental wafer and wine are transformed into actual yet eternal flesh and blood of Christ) and that such substances as the trinity, are beyond all human comprehension—miracles and dogmas to believe in, not propositions to investigate and reason about· as an ancient Father of the church declared: *"Credo quia impossibile."* This renders it something paradoxical that a prince of this Church— and an American one at that—should object to a theory because it is beyond his comprehension. Besides, relativity is not absolutely unintelligible; other men not cardinals do understand it; while the mysteries of the faith are excluded by prescription from all human understanding, lay no less than ecclesiastical.

His Eminence's first reason against relativity, one is led to suspect, served in fact as a rationalization for his second one: that relativity is an explanation which has no need of the hypothesis of God. To the hieratic mind the truth or falsity of the theory, its fertility or barrenness, is irrelevant. If it can dispense with God it is damned together with its maker.

Set beside this elimination of relativity by religious ukase its handling by a scientific opponent. Professor Miller of the Case School of Applied Science, is a distinguished physicist, an expert in his field. He rejects relativity because he holds it to be based on mistaken observation. It is his view that the Michelson-Morley experiment, on which the theory largely depends, failed to establish the absence of a drift in the ether; that consequently there is no ground for rejecting the ether theory. He believes that physics has need of the ether hypothesis and that there really is an ether, but that the devices and methods used to discern its influence were inadequate. What, then, was his course of action? Did he content himself with contradicting the record and, after the manner of the prince of the universal Roman and Apostolic Church, denouncing a theory which dispenses with ether as it does with God? No. Not even charlatans among scientists could be as shameless as that, much less the masters of their fields. Mr. Miller, having examined the record and considered the evidence, sets himself to repeat the basic experiment, to carry it out more completely, more excellently than ever before. He refines his instruments, seeks to establish more harmonious conditions, to improve techniques, and to take more delicate measurements; he took every precaution he could compass against possible errors. He has already laid some findings before his scientific peers. They were apparently as dissatisfied with those as he with the Michelson-Morley findings. Did they denounce and excommunicate him? No. The doubt he roused was welcomed. Professor Michelson himself turned to a new repetition of his famous experiment, with still more favorable conditions, still better instruments and techniques.

However intense and even passionate the disagreement between these men of science or any other, the actions which it animates cannot fail at last to bring about a consensus, the richer, the more stable and certain for the disagreements. Disagreements between men of religion and men of science, or, for that matter, between men of one religion and men of another, are precluded from such a consummation. The Einsteins, the Millers, the Michelsons are interested in truth, whatever its import. They follow the experimental event, no matter where it leads. The Piuses, the Inges, the O'Connells, the Cannons, the Mannings, the religionists of every cult and sect, to the very last modernizer, are given over without recall, each to his ecclesiastical establishment, and they know precisely what that is and teaches. Vested interests of their bodies and minds beyond any withdrawal, the things of the churches shall not fail, the religionists declare. Perforce they hesitate at no means within their power to vindicate that solvency.

Such as the warfare of religion against science is, it appears to be intrinsic to the nature of the faiths that conduct it. They could not make peace if they dared. For on the

whole and in the long run, religion is aware of its own in-
adequacies and fears their consequences. Hence it seems
at least as fully busy about eliminating its competitors as
minding its task. It seems to fear the judgment of the
human spirit should that be able to choose between science
and itself. Most rarely has it the candor and the courage, in
the utterance of such a churchman as the Reverend Mr.
Fosdick, to confess itself that it may be shriven and begin
anew. At their worst, religions continue in the tradition
of the orthodoxies, with their engines of repression, persecution, and elimination. At their best, religions make a
reservation of some perspective of standards, ideals, or
values. These, they say, are taboo to every doubt, sacred
from every inquiry. They are the new carriers of that
unique and insuperable ineffability which is the especial
attribution of religious revelations, and in them now anew
inhere eternally the ultimate distillations of every good that
fate and chance may cast upon the shores of human life.
These new "values" then replace the elder treasures of the
faith, to be defended at all hazards and by every means,
thereby moving the scene of the unfair war against science
to a different level and another field; today it is humanism
and the milder forms of the modernist heresy; yesterday
it was infant damnation and human "perfectibility"; and
who knows what the occasion will bring up tomorrow?

XII

And what else, in the circumstances, is left for religion
to do? To fight without favorable handicaps, fairly, on
equal terms with science, religion would need to relinquish
its pretensions to possess an infallible revelation of the
absolute and eternal, identical amid all change, good
above all evils, the sure salvation at last of every man. It

would need to adopt the tentativeness, the experimental-ism, and the relativism without which science could not be, replacing dogma with hypothesis, commandment with invitation, authority with free co-operation. It would need to concern itself with the perfection of function, not the enforcement of rules admitting of no revision or alteration. It would need to concede that revision and alteration do take place, have taken place, and will go on taking place, of all its eternals and absolutes.

That there is an endeavor after such a consummation the trends in the most liberal churches show. Did not John Morley say long ago that "the next great task of science is to create a new religion for humanity"? And what else is the import of religious humanism? Do not some devotees yearn to make a religion of science itself? But when science becomes a religion, it ceases perforce to be science. It ac-quires first the fixity and dogmatism of religions; then their infallibility and ineffableness; and its virtue as the *pursuit* of the knowledge which is power has departed from it. A fixed and dogmatic science is as ironic as a skeptical and fluid religion. The first has abandoned discovery, the second has become powerless to guarantee salvation.

We are, it would seem, at an impasse.

But perhaps a way out is not required. Perhaps we are strangers elsewhere and the impasse is our home. Perhaps a cessation in the warfare of religion against science would be yet another stagnation in the soul of man. Perhaps the ulti-mate stagnation. "Let us have Peace" is a prayer graven in stone over the door of the mausoleum of a dead general who led a victorious army in a civil war.[2] If man were not, in Job's words, born unto trouble, what would he be born to? If there were no warfare to man upon earth, whatever else could there be to him? Religion and science are opposite

---

[2] General Grant's on Riverside Drive in New York City.

poles of the same energies, like cold and heat or dark and light. Where one is, the other cannot be, so long as the energies are actual, since both present merely locations and degrees of the movement of our vital forces, since both serve but as stances of the total propulsion of our living selves. From the quietness and securities of fixed and frozen faith to the quicknesses and inquiries of mobile, warm doubt and back again, up and down and round and round, our spirits move, all the days of our life. Religion is a frozen asset, paying interest but incapable ever of being reinvested; science is cash forever in circulation, always paying out a new adventure. Religion is security, preoccupied with death; science is the living hazard of the struggle for life itself, the other pole to religion. Let a distance cease to separate these poles and the two come together and be one, this movement ceases also, and life is done. Then unity indeed supervenes, eternity in truth ensues, and immortality in fact sets in. But who cares? For then no longer does any unresting mind remain to think up proofs for these finales, nor any troubled heart survive that should desire them. When they are, man is not, nor any world which he might know and love; when man is, they are not and cannot be. Since only the dead are immortal, only that which has never become is eternal, only the nonexistent is one and the same. Against the sheer blank of this nothingness the thin red line of life thrusts on, manifold, changeful, varied, a warfare and a trouble, division in its works and ways, death at its heart. Of this creative thrust religion and science are as the magnetic poles, not to be joined together while it can carry on.

Freedom and the Artist

I

IN ANY language, the word freedom has a multitude of meanings. These are, as often as not, mutually opposed and contradictory. They elude every endeavor to fuse them into a single, unvarying, self-consistent concept. Soon or late one is led to conclude that consistency and invariancy are the contraries of freedom, that they so work as first to arrest and then to kill off the act of choosing between alternatives, the spontaneous spring and flow of self-differentiation wherein freedom is known. Indeed, the paradoxes of freedom extend so far that even compulsions of outer power may be welcomed as releases from inner restraints. The young Nazi who boasted that his Führer set him free was not lying when, in reply to the question, "Free from what?" he said, "Free from Freedom." The deliberative tension of choosing, the fiat of decision and the sense of release, the feeling of responsibility for the choice, that compenetrate the decision, appear to make up the core of every man's existence and constitute the initiation and ending of his struggle to live. At this core, he stands willy-nilly on his own feet, naked, alone, projecting the chart of his own stark purpose into the unchartable future at his own stark risk, and taking the consequences with his own strength. Nature, it appears, provides relaxations from this state of our essential being of which the prototype is sleep and the finality death, and a man's spirit welcomes them as the dropping of a burden. But the inwardness of the burden is the man's life and his liberty.

Now, when he was an infant, his mother or his father took much of the weight of the load from him; and in remembrance, as a grown man he is apt to welcome the teacher or preacher or führer who promises to relieve him in the same way, announcing commandments that admit no alternatives, that he can obey without thinking and act on without choosing. Such commandments unburden him of the tension of choice and decision. They bring the strain of living close to the effortless automatism of sleep. For the time being the man enjoys what William James describes as a moral holiday. Having no choices, he has no responsibilities and no struggles. He surrenders all those to his führer or his God and he feels free.

This is the liberty which the classical world most clearly understood and envisaged; it is the liberty of primitive societies, rationalized in form and perfected in idea as Plato rationalized and perfected it, as the Stoics and the church fathers interpreted it. Its substance is the feeling of relief that comes with relaxation of effort, the sense of ease and comfortable fluency of fitting into a preordained pattern of thought and action and doing willingly what must be done anyhow. It goes with the dissolution of some singularity of effort or resistance in oneself into conformity with institutional requirements. To the outsider it looks like submission, obedience, self-enslavement. But to inner awareness it is an experience of self-liberation. "Thy will, not mine, be done," because doing my will is so terrible and exhausting an effort, is such a strain, such a misery to my being! Let God, then, suffer this freedom, let the Duce, let the Führer! *En la sua voluntade e nostra pace,* and I choose never again to choose; I choose always thereafter to submit my will to his. Thus, by freely choosing servitude, I free myself from the pang and the burden of free will, from the tragedy of choice! Like a free man voluntarily getting himself jailed, I give up freedom for security: I give up choice, variation, and their risks for the assurance of repetition and conformity.

Now free societies frown upon this kind of freedom. They hold it to be illusory, and the choice of it a momentary violation of one's own nature. In his essay *On Liberty*, John Stuart Mill points out that such a choice is a free act which puts an end to all subsequent free acts, and therefore cannot be sanctioned by the laws. Institutional conformity can and often does facilitate personal freedom, as is attested by the difference in this respect between the unmarried and married women in Mediterranean countries. In totalitarian societies, moreover, the conformity goes with the release of an indefinite variety of drives which a free man keeps in leash in a free society where he is responsible for himself to himself, as well as to his neighbors. As the Nazi record shows, this conformity enables him to lust, to kill, to spy, to betray, to boast, without risk and without responsibility. He is truly freed from freedom.

But if he no more needs to make choices, the strain of doing so falls the more heavily upon his masters, who must do the choosing for him. And an elemental aspect of the rule of the masters is the creation and employment of complex instruments of coercion of the very individuals who have sought freedom by surrendering their minds and hearts to the providence of the magisterial will. The record shows that the surrender is never once for all; that it must be itself continually renewed by a new act of choice; that variation from the *credere, obedire e combatere* of the Fascist prescription keeps occurring spontaneously; that to shut out and cut off these variations, the masters need the devices of inquisition, index, excommunication and interdict, secret police, mutual suspicion and denunciation, and all the other instruments of economic, political, and ecclesiastical coercion that history tells of.

Thus the reality of the spontaneities and variations and choices which totalitarianisms shut out is affirmed and vindicated by the activities of that which shuts them out: Freedom repressed in one direction expresses itself in another, and regularly outwits and wears away whatever would nullify it. This is why, in spite of all sophisticated discussions about rights, democratic societies are disposed to hold freedom to be, in the language of the Declaration of Independence, one of the "unalienable rights," equally unalienable in all men however different each may be from the others. Thomas Jefferson, indeed, had written *inherent* and *unalienable,* but the Congress had rejected the word *inherent. Inherent,* nevertheless, properly belongs with *unalienable.*

II

These words, as Jefferson employed them, were intended to signify that liberty is a constitutive element of our being, that it belongs to human nature as the angles and sides of a triangle belong to the triangle. It is from this meaning that our conception of the task and organization of free society and its institutions derives. The liberty, together with the life, the pursuit of happiness, and the other unalienable rights of individuals are the starting points and the continuing goals of social organization. Associations of individuals such as the family, the state, the church, the school, the economic establishment, or the scientific enterprise are but means and instruments "to secure these rights." The powers of government they rightly hold are acquired, secondary, alienable; not inherent, primary, and unalienable. They derive from "the consent of the gov-

131

erned." Their sanction is their works and consequences, not their inward natures. They may—according to their effect for the equal, inherent, and unalienable life, liberty, and pursuit of happiness of different people—be sustained, developed, altered, reorganized, or entirely withdrawn by those people, be they a man and a woman in a family, partners in a business, communicants in a church, citizens in a state, or associates in any other kind of organization.

Such is the ideal of free society implied by the Declaration of Independence. This is what the democracies of the world endeavor, each in its way, to realize by means of their constitutions and to give force and form to, in their different cultural disciplines. This is the ultimate intent of what has vaguely come to be known as "The Four Freedoms." It is to acknowledge, to believe in, and to fight for the right of a person to be the master of the powers of his own body and his own spirit, to be self-possessing and self-possessed; to count, in the company of other men, as one and never as less than one. It is to acknowledge, to believe in, and to fight for the right of individuals to their individuality, their right *to be different* without penalty and without privilege, especially without penalty. It is, in sum, to insure to each man his independence of body and spirit.

In the history of liberty this ideal has been the drive of the constant warfare against slavery; against one person's being at the disposition of another by law; against the subjection of wives and sisters and daughters who so long had no rights that any father or husband or brother need respect; against property in human beings whether black or white; against second-class status or outlawry of men or women because their religions were different; against immobilizing the bodies of men by imposing on them an unchangeable status in society, or immobilizing the minds of men by an unalterable belief in religion.

132

III

Logically and practically, the immobilization of body reduces to the immobilization of mind. Psychologically and historically, the Four Freedoms, wherein these fixations are rejected in 1945 as the Declaration rejected them in 1776, reduce to one. This one is freedom of thought, of inquiry; and this is worthless unless it goes with freedom of expression. Thought is impossible without expression; thought *is* expression; an unexpressed thought, like an unlaid egg, comes to nothing. Given this freedom, then, other freedoms follow. For free thought is creative thought. It is thought of the artist, the thinker, the inventor, the entrepreneur, as they exercise their free initiative. It is thought which varies and multiplies, which spontaneously generates that economy of abundance in ideas which is the indispensable preliminary to abundance in things. Thus, during the so-called ages of faith, differences of belief were harshly penalized; thought was kept bound. Ideas were consequently scarce, and the economy of scarcity in ideas made an economy of scarcity in all the arts: industrial, intellectual, and fine. It restricted production of tools, goods, and services and penalized consumption. The effective initiation of free thought came as new and different ideas about the prosperous management of human relations to superhuman beings—gods, angels, devils, the souls of the dead—by means of the various ceremonials, rituals, relics, sacred texts, and other instruments of negotiation with the supernatural. From this came the ways and works of the Humanists. That with which they enriched the domain of ideas set going an increasing abundance in the domain of things. When thought, acting freely, extended its field from the works of man to the processes of nature, it brought to birth the doctrines and disciplines of scientific method;

and these, applied, led to the invention and perfection of new machines, to increased mastery over soil and sea, plant life, and animal life. They transformed, as they still transform, ancient barrens of nature into modern natural resources, the dead residue of human fabrication into the raw material of new production. Everywhere they trans-value waste into wealth; everywhere they expand scarcity into abundance. Applied to the relations of men to men, they lead to the realization of the primacy of freedom and to the conception of the democratic way of life, with its affirmation that equal liberty is the natural right of the mul-titudes of different men; that it is not the limited, divinely granted prerogative of a few similar by birth, rank, station, and religion. Thus the western world has moved, and the remainder has followed after, from freedom of thought and expression toward freedom of worship and freedom from want and from fear.

Freedom of thought and expression is not only the semi-nal freedom, the initiation, the surge and spring to all the others, it is also their discipline and their test. Where it does not obtain, alternatives cannot come to attention; and if they do come to attention, cannot be criticized, tested, or altered on their merits. Where it does not obtain, no ground can be rationally sought and established for choosing be-tween incompatibles of beauty or use, be they forms or faiths, ends or means, for they cannot be brought together on equal terms and compared on equal terms, and only such comparisons lead to the knowledge which is power. Where it is prevented, decision regarding which idea to abandon and which to fight for is then a helpless gesture, a blow without force, a will without power. Freedom of thought and expression is, thus, the first and the last insur-ance of human individuality against the tyrannies and in-ertias of state, church, business enterprise, institution of

134

learning, academy of art, or any other vested interest of the cultural economy of mankind.

IV

What, now, is this freedom in any one man's thought? What are its stigmata? How does he know he has it? How can he communicate his knowledge to others? I am not sure that it can be communicated at all by means of words. Freedom, more than any other experience, is what William James used to call "knowledge of acquaintance," that is, an immediate experience which cannot be transposed into the concepts of which words are primarily the incarnations. Words may converge toward the experience, point it like a pointer-dog, center on it, but neither express it nor communicate it. What they capture, if they capture anything, is the dead fowl, not the living bird. They do not catch it in the act of life.

Let the reader, if he will, make an experiment. Let him try to catch his own freedom in the act of reading. What is his situation? Obviously his will, his purpose, is set upon an object, his attention has a center, and his center presumably consists of the idea these pages of words purport to convey to him. It is one item in an indefinite, wider, deeper stream of his consciousness. In this stream there flow together and suffuse one another all sorts of impressions and expressions, actions and passions, stimulations and responses. From the the world which surrounds his body there come to his eyes perceptions of his room and of all the objects it contains, their shapes, their colors, their relations to one another; there come to his ears the endless multiplicity and variety of sounds; to his nose come odors, scents, stenches, fragrances, bouquets, smells, and stinks; to his tongue and palate tastes, flavors, textures soft or

135

sharp, stinging or smooth, harsh or gentle, from the entire world around him, but notably from people, from food, drink, tobacco, talcum; and if he smokes while he reads there come the poignant consolations of the smoker's fumes. The rest of his body reacts to the texture, the hardness and softness of the chair he sits on, the table he sits by, the variations of warmth and cold in the surrounding air. At the same time these outer events set going inner changes. They awaken associations. They arouse memories. They initiate shifts of his body's posture, alterations in the tempo of the circulation of his blood, his breathing, his differential organic tensions. And all these happenings together concur into a single stream in which each remains distinct but not separate from the others, in which each is inside the others as the tones of a tune are inside each other. When the reader is aware of this compenetration and togetherness, when he is sensitive to each but exclusively conscious of none, his state is akin to reverie. His consciousness flows without direction and none of its waves feels more important than any other. An undirected stream, it is at the same time a matrix and spring of spontaneities. The multitudinous events it consists of diversify, separately and together. They compose concords and discords, mutual facilitations and obstructions. When obstructions reach a certain intensity, a strength singular to the individuality of the reader, he passes from the state like reverie, into a state of active thinking. His consciousness takes on direction. His mind assumes a gradient. One item, out of the multitudinous variety, becomes the new object of its attention. It minds that object. Minding that object is not, however, a simple, smooth activity; it is a complex strenuous struggle in the half-dark. It consists in concurrently heightening attention to the object, and in breaking through, shutting out, cutting off, and leaving behind the unceasing solicitation of the alternatives and competitors whose impacts rain from all the senses and all the memories. If the effort is successful, a decision has occurred; the sense of labor, of strain and struggle and squeeze is followed by a feeling of effortless regard. The reader's mind takes in the pages of words as by an untrammeled movement on an open road; the idea he pursues becomes ever more clear and distinct, the pursuit ever more relaxed and powerful, powerful and delightful; even if the material is familiar, it feels new; it brings repristination and surprise; unprecedented thoughts and images fill his ken—until alternatives crowd again, and the struggle is repeated at a more complex level with a diversified direction.

Perhaps the poor words I have just set down may lead the reader to perceive reading as the experience of freedom it sometimes can be, or to realize the freedom in some other activity of his own. In its naked dynamic this freedom seems regularly to be a choice between alternatives already given, or the evocation of new and unprecedented alternatives not to be anticipated or foretold. Sometimes both processes concur. Each—the one, the decision between options already given, the consenting to one, the dissenting from its competitor; the other, the bringing to birth of some diversification, singular, new, and ungiven—is creative. The tension of it is an irreducible immediate experience and discourse about it falls into disputes and contradictions. Albert Einstein gave his own summary of it at a dinner in honor of Max Planck: "This daily striving," he said, "is dictated by no principle or program, but arises from immediate personal need. The emotional condition which renders possible such achievements is like that of the religious devotee or lover." . . . The impulse to grapple problems is like a "demoniac possession."

V

Traditionally, the process just sky-lined is regarded as the singularity of genius, which as Jacques Louis David declared, "is the duty of the artist." But if the line is indicative, the process is "inherent and unalienable" in all men. In the artist, however, it stands out; in the artist it is so conspicuous that it has come to be regarded as the signature of his vocation, the singularity of his being the kind of man he is, his duty, as David said. James Joyce gave the ineluctable urge to be free an ultimate expression. He wrote at the end of his *Portrait of the Artist as a Young Man,*

I will not serve that in which I no longer believe, whether it call itself my home, my fatherland or my church; and I will try to express myself as freely as I can and as wholly as I can, using for my defense the only arms I allow myself to use, silence, exile and cunning.

I do not fear to be alone or to be spurned for another, or to leave whatever I have to leave. And I am not afraid to make a mistake, even a great mistake, a lifelong mistake, and perhaps as long as eternity, too.

And why this uttermost renunciation and risk and suppression? Because the Artist chose, against all that he rejected, "to discover a way of life or art where his spirit could express itself in unfettered fredom." In his immediate personal impulse he had come to a decision, not "moral" but deeper, more urgent than any "moral" prescription could be, to affirm the singularity of his vision, and to achieve its utterance regardless of what it might cost him. All artists, I think, each in his kind and degree, make such decisions, decisions which demonstrate freedom. And it is this freedom of the artist that is also the aboriginal freedom of the psyche of man which homes and fatherlands and churches and all the institutional and vested interests of civilization

fear more than any other. It is because in the artist this freedom is more potent, less checked and overlaid than in other
men that institutional authority is always attacking the
artist.

We ask, then, *why?* What is there in the artist, considered
as the vessel of freedom, to make him more dangerous for
established interests than the scientist or inventor or religious prophet? Each is in his own characteristic way a vessel of freedom, and the establishments wherein their singularity lives and moves and has its being owe their existence
to an act of freedom, a variation from something older, an
initiation of something altogether new. This is the establishment's dynamic at birth, its center of power while it
grows up, its enshrined idol when it has grown old. This is
the ancient mystery on which it bases its claim to authority.
Thus, in religion it comes as revelation, challenging all
existing beliefs, winning its way among them not by privilege but on merit. In the course of time the prophet to
whom the revelation has been directly revealed dies. To
his successors it is no longer the direct original word of
God. It is not something that they themselves hear, but
something which they are told, and believe, that another
man has heard; a deposit of faith, no longer the revelation
but the tradition of the generations; and they claim authority for it by virtue of an authorship far away and long
ago. In science, again, the new insight, the fresh explanation, the unpredictable law, comes to the scientist as his
images come to the artist; it acts upon his discipline as the
initiation of a new ordering of his observations and instruments, the ground of a new system with new devices and
methods. The same thing holds for the inventor. The
moment when he decides upon his unprecedented variation, upon a machine or a method, is the moment of freedom, of originality, initiation, innovation. The trials and

tests, the elaborations and development which then follow are analogous to reorganization in the sciences, to tradition in religion. They are derivative and consequential, not primary. The primary event is the deciding perception, the initiating act of freedom. In this respect, then, artist, prophet, scientist, and inventor are brothers under the skin. All are equally artists.

Here, however, the resemblance stops. The productions of saints or prophets, of men of science and of inventors, to be authentic, are subject to external checks and conformations. Scientists, and to a lesser degree inventors, are more finders than makers, more discoverers than creators. Artists are entirely creators. A great astronomer like Ptolemy, a great chemist like Willard Gibbs, a great mathematician like Albert Einstein is truly a man of genius; artistic originality cannot be denied him. But what he achieves does not depend primarily on what he is in himself, on his authentic essence. His ideas are intended to account for a world independent of himself, at which he looks and upon which he reflects. This world was there before he was and will remain when he no longer is. The material of which he treats is an ever-present material which, as best he can, he manipulates, breaking it up into little bits (this is called analysis) and putting the bits together in divers ways (this is called synthesis), all the time striving, searching, seeking, not for something which is not there and never was there, but for something which he believes was always there and will always be there; something which, should he fail to find it, another surely will. Let us suppose that the Nazis had done the worst they can in their assault upon the human race. Suppose that they had destroyed all the libraries and museums and laboratories of the entire world; suppose that they had extirpated the collective memory of mankind. Suppose that they had wiped out the entire

140

record of man's insights into nature, of his power over nature. Suppose that they had also reduced to dust and ashes the free personal expressions of the human spirit in music, letters, and the graphic and plastic arts. Nevertheless, the subject matter of the sciences, which is the indestructible stuff of the natural world, would still be there, as available as it ever was: and physics, chemistry, astronomy, and the other sciences could still be re-created. Free thought, reacting to the natural scene, could not fail sooner or later to elicit whatever the past has discerned and formulated about the scene, and much more beside. But what could it recover of the music and poetry and drama and painting and sculpture and architecture that had been destroyed? These are wholly the works of man, creatures of his singularity, not echoes or images of a nature other than himself. Once lost, with all remembrance gone, what chance is there that they may be restored?

Or, for that matter, that the lost and forgotten images and vessels and instruments and literature of the churches be recovered? For religion, too, lacks the outward base of the sciences. Not only its ikons and idols, its vestments and symbols and rituals, but also the speculations of its dogmatic theologians, their ideas of the supernatural and their rationalizing elaborations of those ideas, live closer to the arts than to the sciences. Once lost, a cultus is irrecoverable. Its springs are in the impulsion of men, not in the necessary connections of nature, and how it expresses those impulsions is a contingency of fortune, not a determination of law. In each and every cultus the differential is arbitrary, original, and singular, truly a revelation of grace, which once forgotten is lost and never likely to be repeated. Because of this character of their faiths, it has been the consistent practice of churches to guard their deposits of faith by demanding both exclusive authority over the education

141

which carries memory of the past from one generation to another, and power to shut out and cut off every variation, every novelty which might oppose a new authenticity to the old authority. Thus, once a divinity has been revealed and his cultus established, his devotees become the enemies of all other originality and authorship. Liberty is reduced simply to *libertas obedientiae*. While the bounds to the freedom of the scientist and the inventor is the process of nature, the check upon the freedom of the religionist is the arrest of process by the vested interests of human nature.

Neither of these circumstances so operate on the artist. They surround, but neither bound nor check his freedom. They may occasion or sustain or oppose his creativity, but they do not cause it. A maker, but neither a finder nor discoverer nor repeater, the artist stands as unique, the cause of that which he makes. His work cannot be unless he himself has been. His relationship to it has the inevitability of a mother's to the child she bears. And his work is somehow his fiat as a child cannot be. For illustration, consider the works of Leonardo, that *uomo universale* who was at one and the same time a mathematician, a scientist and inventor, and an artist. The many notebooks he has left have long been objects of precise and loving scrutiny. They reveal him an anatomist who dissected at least thirty corpses, a physiologist who studied and drew embryos at various stages of development, and who made the first accurate drawings of the interior organs. He is said to have anticipated Harvey's discovery of the circulation of the blood. The notebooks reveal him also as a city planner, a civil and sanitary engineer, an architect who constructed relief maps of Italy and laid out an astronomical observatory, a student of the heavens who opposed astrology and a student of the earth who decried alchemy. He devised and planned

142

cranes, borers, armored tanks, spinning machines, flying machines. Much of his finding in the field of science and invention had been banned. But all of it sooner or later was repeated by other men of science and invention, was done better, and advanced farther. His paintings, on the other hand, remain unique. Their authenticity is personal to him, is irrecoverable, and not reproducible by another. His *Trattato della pittura* contains everything and communicates everything but the quality which makes Leonardo's work Leonardo's. Had the Nazis destroyed *Mona Lisa* or *The Last Supper*, these paintings would have been lost forever. They could not be repeated. For each, like a living child, is the unique effect of a unique cause. The child is born once and never again. And so also are the creations of the artist. There is a sense in which each such creation is an original act, a direct perception, a decision whose authority is in itself and in nothing else beside: in a word, a liberty taken and an idea made free. Leonardo was fully aware of the indefeasible authenticity of such perceptions and decisions, and he was skeptical of ecclesiasticism, of its dogmas about nature and the supernatural, and of its techniques for manipulating the supernatural. "Whoever," he wrote, "in discussion adduces authority, uses not his intellect but memory." In a world not too hospitable to free thought, he found ways to vindicate this liberty of the artist: "When besieged by ambitious tyrants, I find a means of defense wherewith to preserve the chief gift of nature, which is liberty." The means, basically, was to exercise the creative imagination of the artist; to preserve liberty, that is, keeping it alive and active at the source; by functioning as the unique cause of his singular effects.

And is not the same thing true of all artists, whatever their arts? Could the compositions of Bach or Mozart or Beethoven or Debussy or Gershwin have existed if their

authors had not existed? Once the works do come into existence virtuosos and amateurs can perform them again and
again; critics can talk about them; a theory and practice of
music, a musicology or science of music which has them for
their subject-matter can follow. But without them, repetition and discourse are as fantastic as a biography of an unborn man, which would be knowledge about nobody at all.
If, however, the biography did not pretend to a subject
matter, but came simply as a free act of an artist's imagination, it would give knowledge of acquaintance, it would
become itself the subject matter for the critic, the scientist,
and the student. It would be an authentic work of art, and
its values would start in itself and return to itself. It would
become one more inhabitant of the world of the arts, which
those that enter must encounter and respond to and therefore learn.

VI

Now all such works as Leonardo's *Trattato* or Schön-
berg's studies of harmony, or any of the records, that endeavor to communicate the *How*, the *What*, and the *Why*
of the arts, are supposed to function as aids to learning.
They operate as the middlemen between the past and the
future, the facilitators of tradition, the enablers of knowledge and skill. Not so long ago writers on art set this knowledge and skill over against originality, and opposed
inspiration—which is free and not to be controlled—to art
—which is workmanship and therefore all control. Today,
writers on art recognize that workmanship and control
are also fields for inspiration, and that in contemporary
painting, for example, the momentous choices concern the
what far less than the *how;* the art is all in the artistry. The
originality, the authentic innovation of the artists, consists, however, in the way they vary from the past, not in

the way they repeat it. But how can they be sure not to repeat the past if they do not know the past, if the past of their art is not alive in them as the past of their growing bodies is alive in their bodies and being taken up into the future?

The past of his art is the artist's peculiar social and institutional inheritance. It is given in his tools, materials and mediums, in the creations of past masters and the precepts of present teachers. It is that which colleges and art schools and music schools are able to communicate and therefore that which authority requires the artist shall repeat. State, school, business establishment, church, particularly church, say to the artist: "Be ye perfect even as your fathers before you were perfect. Say today what they said yesterday. Say it in the same way. Or if you must vary, we permit you, within reason, a certain liberty in *how* you say it, but never in *what* you say." This attitude of authority has had its influence upon the artist's emphasis upon *technique* as against *theme*. Thus the drama of salvation and its agonists are an invariant subject matter of Christian art. In its pictorial utterance it alters from the hieroglyphlike statement of the Byzantines to the human amplitudes of Leonardo, to the distortions of El Greco. The eye of churchly authority sees the *what* of each painter as the same dictate that it had been from the days of St. Basil. The secular eye, however, sees the being and meaning of that *what* as suffused and transformed by the *hows;* Leonardo, El Greco, the Byzantines do *not* say the same thing. Theme, material, and media serve as occasions and vehicles for the painter's freedom, and the better he knows them, the greater the liberties he can take with them.

And so it is in all the arts. Their practitioners may employ or reject the deliverances of the past, but only on the penalty of merely repeating them may they ignore them. Those deliverances are at once the field and discipline of

inspiration, the channel by which choices and new forms
come to expression, the flesh that incarnates the idea which
the imagination creates. Without this deliverance originality is but blind freedom, undirected spontaneity such as that
of Epicurus' atoms, or of the waves of the stream of consciousness. The ancestral skills and knowledges of which
the deliverance is the carry-over and compenetration provide originality with its point of departure. Had Stephen
Collins Foster not been as aware as he was of Mozart and
Beethoven and Rossini and Schubert and Donizetti, he
could not have been as American as he is. Benny Goodman
is a clarinetist no less compelling than the crooner Frank
Sinatra. The youth of the nation are his devotees. He is
one of the guys that gives and gives and evokes from all the
tribes of Bobby-sock and Hep-cat a correspondingly
greater outpouring so that they cut the rug to beat the
band. The other day the distinguished virtuoso lectured
to the Juilliard School of Music. He told the students:
"Every one needs a solid classical basis before they can
embark on jazz." And to illustrate the dictum he made
hearts swing by improvising freely on Brahms.

There is a modern delusion, cultivated by the lazy and
the arty, that originality is the prerogative of ignorance.
Nothing could be farther from the facts of record. Ignorance is the enemy of originality. Knowledge is the field of
freedom, of choice, decision, new expression. The larger
the field, the richer the chances of originality, whether it
comes to utterance by way of selections and rejections,
combinations and mutations, or spontaneous variations.
Knowledge is the mind's economy of abundance. Inspiration receives its occasion and opportunity, freedom its
enhancement, according to the number and variety and patterns of the data amid which it occurs. It is this fact which
renders museums, orchestras, schools, galleries important

146

to the freedom of the artist when he desires to cultivate his liberty, and dangerous when authority seeks to police and imprison it. It is this fact which brings folk art naturally near to the spontaneities of great artists. It is why sects and cults and schools which aim only to cultivate a particular and exclusive expression and cut off and shut out alternatives usually turn out to be so barren. Inspiration springs more readily from knowledge than from ignorance; knowledge is the food and drink of originality in the arts as well as in the sciences.

But in the arts, the individual expression, the singularity of the artist's utterance, is autonomous, self-referent, an absolute in the only sense that the word can have practical bearing. The artist's images and ideas are truly firsts, truly new beginnings, that are born into a world not made for them, in which their survival is the issue of a struggle wherein victory is not guaranteed in advance. As they first take shape in his fantasy, their very being is a tentative, a hint indefinitely articulate, a line here, a phrase there, a cadence elsewhere, given body in notation after notation, sketch after sketch, and worked out first as a drawing, a painting, a blueprint, a score, or a poem, or a talk. For that matter this holds of scientific ideas and inventions, too. They also begin as free acts of the imagination. Should they never reach verification by experiment and by incarnation in things and tools and human relations, they, too, would be countable as works of art. All such works generate outer consequences. Their autonomy is truly creative; they are in fact what the philosopher means by *idées forces*. They have the power to turn the minds and hearts of men in new directions, toward new interests, new forms, new meanings; sometimes they transvalue the manners and morals of a generation.

147

VII

Poets and philosophers have always been aware of the consequential power of the artist's initiative, and some have glorified it and claimed for the artist a commensurate privilege, whereas others have feared and denounced it and have undertaken either to tame his originality and harness it up, or have outlawed him from society altogether. This initiative is what Plato called inspiration as opposed to art. As manifest through the poet, Plato held it to be an anarchic and disruptive agency which blasphemed the gods and corrupted youth. He banished it from his ideal society. An early nineteenth-century echo of his, the poet Thomas Love Peacock, described the poetry of his time as resolvable into "the rant of unregulated passion, the whining of exaggerated feeling, and the cant of factitious sentiment"; the poet was "a semi-barbarian in a civilized community." Per contra, his friend and patron, the poet Shelley, who wrote a *Defence* against Peacock's attack, declared the poet, and in him every artist in his kind and degree, to be the vehicle of a mighty power "of communicating and receiving intense and impassioned conceptions respecting man and nature," a power artists might fight even while they serve it. "Poets are the hierophants of an unapprehended inspiration; the mirrors of the gigantic shadow which futurity cases upon the present; . . . The influence which is moved not but moves. Poets are the unacknowledged legislators of the world." A generation after Shelley's *Defence* was published, Walt Whitman described "the divine literatus" as succeeding the priest; "standing apart from all else . . . sole and untouchable by any canons of authority or any rules derived from precedent, state-safety, the acts of legislatures or even from what is called religion, modesty or art"; causing with his new

148

ideas and new expressions "changes, growth, removal greater than the longest and bloodiest wars or the most stupendous merely dynastic or commercial overturn." And may it not be said that poets such as Voltaire or Rousseau, painters such as Jacques Louis David, musicians such as Beethoven or Debussy or Wagner, to name only obvious instances, did in fact turn thoughts in new directions, toward new images and conceptions, and gave new shapes to things? It is not merely that artists make visible the invisible, bring absent objects to present preception; that like Kipling, Jules Verne, H. G. Wells, Edgar Poe, they make images of a future which events turn into true prophecies; it is also that artists forefigure the shape of things to come because the figures which their imagination shapes so work as to cause them to come.

The impact of the artist's innovation on society, then, is that of a challenging and transforming power. It springs from his freedom and throughout the ages testifies to this freedom. Not the least significant of its operations is the fact that it tends to keep the artist a free man in general society and serves to make societies of artists free societies; the fact that poet and painter and sculptor and musician, patronized as they may be, come throughout recorded history to move in the circles of the kings and nobles and emperors, their betters, as the equals of those betters. Alike in the palace, the salon, the coffee house, or the club, the invidious distinctions which shut men of other occupations out, fall away where the artist is concerned. And in their own associations artists come together not on the basis of rank or station or faith or color or wealth, but on the basis of personal competency and common interest. As Benny Goodman recently said, when asked how it happened that he had both Negro and white musicians in his band: "I'm trying to play good music first of all. I'm not trying to solve

149

any problems. No musician is any good to me unless he's a good musician. You work with a man because he's a good man—that's all. Honestly, I'm not a do-gooder. I'm just a musician."

What this one of the truly creative artists of our generation has said expresses the ethos authentic to art. It is the ethos of freedom, which uncompromisingly detaches the integrity of the author, his sovereignty over his creation, from the institutions of the civilization amid which he lives, moves, and struggles to maintain his being as a free man. In the economy of his community he is only a small businessman, an independent entrepreneur who, at his own risk, produces as he inwardly must, and markets his productions as he outwardly can. His calling, hence, is subject to all the pressures and solicitations that the forces which define the market—church, state, school, business enterprise, political party, and other vested interests of society—can bring to bear upon it. Their end and their purpose are that the artist shall abandon his proper ethos and conform to theirs. Conservative and liberal alike would rather have him speak *for* them than *to* them. They feel his independence as a danger and a challenge. Ultimately they fear his freedom and would prostitute or destroy it. So they undertake to belittle and condemn it. There was conservative Plato, who considered the painter to be as inferior to the carpenter as the carpenter is to God; to whom Homer, that "master and leader of tragedy" was the fabricator of imitations of imitations, a corrupter of youth who stirs but their passions and makes them sympathetic to evil. There was Diderot, in many respects Plato's opposite, who saw art as only the vehicle of civil and social philosophy. Plato and Diderot are representative spokesmen of the prevailing view of the arts: that they should either be as servants and voices of the state or should not be at all.

Often, the ethos of the artist and the ethos of the community flow together and are one. Then the artist does in fact express the civil and social intent. But this at-oneness is neither identity nor subjection, it is spontaneous participation and voluntary agreement; the artist remains as independent as he was before. The hopes and fears of the community, its work and play, its rejections and affirmations, its spirit, its ruling passion may be that pattern among multitudinous alternatives of an artist's environment which spontaneously touches off his imagination, so that he brings it to utterance in symbols and figures that his sect or his people or his age find right and take up to be the vehicle of their spirit, the torch which their runners hand on, generation to generation. Their schools, their public buildings, their museums then conserve, repeat, and transmit them; they figure in the ceremonials and sacraments of the common life; they are displayed, invoked, or quoted in celebrations of triumph and in times of danger, until they have lost their relevancy and new symbols displace them. Thus the Greeks used Homer and the other poets; thus the Judeo-Christian cultists used the psalmists and the prophets, and so on.

Sometimes no new symbols are created, but old symbols are revived, modified, and put to new uses, as was the case during the generation before the French Revolution. From that generation the humanities, which had gone dead in the schools, received new life by being employed as the vehicles and symbols of the idea of liberty; the works of Livy, Sallust, Plutarch, and Tacitus were made the carriers of the ethos of the French democrats. The heroes and martyrs of republican Rome became the painters' and sculptors' symbols of Frenchmen's self-dedication to liberty. The ethos of David's *Oath of the Horatii,* for example, was not contained in the images it presented but in the ideals they represented. This observation receives an ironical re-enforcement from the fact that not so very long ago *L'Action française* advocated a revival of Latin studies for Vichy French youth as a means of recovering the Roman disposition toward hierarchy and privilege.

Sometimes an artist's expression of his community's feeling or spirit remains more personal to him than vocal of his community. Vision of the latter's crisis and need, it achieves a momentary harmony with its awareness, or perhaps none at all. Such seems to have been the case with the harsh, disturbing panels in which Thomas Benton responded, shortly after Pearl Harbor, to the Japanazi horrors. The ethos of Irving Berlin's song "My British Buddy" had a longer duration. It was first sung in London in November 1943, a lyric interpolated in the book of *This Is the Army*. It was sung at a time when the irritations, the tensions, and strains following the location of millions of American soldiers among the British, had reached a certain climax. The resulting sentiment alike among the British and among the Americans was confused but explosive. Of this sentiment Berlin's "lyric" became at once the symbol, the expression, and the catharsis.

I arrived in London
Just the other day
Speaking to a soldier
From the U.S.A.
He told me of the Army life he
led
And speaking of the British
boys, he said:
We're as different as can be.
He thinks he's winning the war
And I think it's me.
But we're in there pitching
And on one thing we agree:

When the job is done
And the war is won
We'll be clasping hands across
the sea.
My British buddy
We're as different as can be.
I like my coffee and rolls
And he likes his tea.
But we're in there pitching
Till we get to Germany.
When we've licked the Hun
And the Japs are done
We'll be clasping hands across
the sea.

These verses may not be the best of poetry, but their social relevance was instant, spontaneous, and complete. They crystallized an emotion, purged, and relieved it. For a while everybody in England was singing them.

Now what an artist responds to and how he responds is not in the power of society. Ethos happens; it can be neither bought nor commanded. As the barren records of so many official painters and sculptors and poets laureate demonstrate, the best an institution can do is provide conditions favorable to its happening. To continue with modern instances, this is what General Somervell, head of the service of supply of the American War Deparment, had tried to do. As director of the Works Progress Administration of New York during the great depression, he had learned that while artists must live if they are to practice their art, that which they produce and how they produce it is not to be conformed to the conditions of their earning a living. He saw the value, for the morale of the armed forces and the ethos of the nation at war, of a pictorial record of the life of battle on sea and land. With the War Department's Advisory Committee on Art to counsel him, he arranged to send painters and others to the various theatres of war. Owing to Representative Starnes of Alabama, the hundred thousand dollars allocated to this undertaking was cut from the war budget. That General Somervell's social wisdom was not entirely nullified is due to a commercial firm which, for its own purposes, of course, as well as for the sake of the national morale and the national culture, took over the project. The Navy has been able to do what Congress refused the Army. If the productions which are the fruit of both appear so far not to have caught the public imagination, they do communicate the authentic expressions of the personal decisions of different American artists regarding the quality, the character, and the meaning of that which they have been asked to tell about; they do present the signature of the each painter's singularity. Should the public to which their works are addressed take one of them to heart, see it as the figure of its own vision, and hear it as the voice of its own passion; should the people orchestrate this creation to the older symbols of their common spirit, they will have given it the ethos it is naturally without. Always ethos accrues to a work of art when the singularity it expresses is spontaneously transfigured into a symbol of common meanings and emotions. The work's conformity then is a free happening, not a required fitting, and its ethos becomes a significance likely to last.

VIII

That this identification of private expression with public meanings which we call ethos must be spontaneous and uncoerced is just as true for authoritarian as for free societies. The endeavor to impose identity, to make conformation coercive is, however, institutional and it seems as inveterate as art itself. We call it censorship. It consists in procrustean prescriptions of what shall be expression and what shall not be expression, and often of how it shall be expressed and how it shall not be expressed. It is dictatorship over the content and methods of the arts, and it is effective dictatorship in the degree that the censors have power to control the media of communication. The inquisitors of an earlier age undertook to control also thinking itself and the Japanese of today have the unique distinction of punishing men and women for thinking, without uttering, "dangerous thoughts." The metaphysical grounding and moral justification of censorship go back, of course, to Plato who, presuming that it is possible to attain certain and infallible knowledge of the nature of the best state and of the

154

best man, argued that poetry—and by implication, all the arts—must conform to these perfections and communicate only them, and that therefore it was the duty of authority to police the arts. What in Plato was philosophical speculation became in the hierarchs of the Roman Catholic establishment, theological dogma; the certain and infallible knowledge which to Plato was only possible became to them actual as Revelation, the deposit of faith entrusted by God into their keeping. The canon law actually prescribes the policing of the arts which the Platonic dialogues such as the *Republic* and the *Laws* only justify. Since, in the clerical eye, art is to the church as the humanity of Jesus is to his divinity, it is the duty of the clergy to see that artists conform to the laws of the church. One of these requires bishops to safeguard traditional forms. Another forbids the approval of images contrary to custom. A third requires that robes, furniture, and other articles of churchly use must conform to liturgical description, ecclesiastical tradition, and the law of religious art. In 1932, when the new Pinakothek was dedicated at the Vatican, the Pope then ruling, Pius XI, took occasion to define the Church's stand on whatever differs from the authorized requirements. The effect was to cut off and shut out the different. Art being a means of salvation, nothing that might distract the faithful from this goal could be permitted—the primitive, the grotesque, the caricaturelike are ruled out. So also is the modern mode in architecture. Art in the church must keep to the venerable tradition and develop it. Its artists must adhere to *formae a traditione receptae*. Their freedom, in sum, can be only *libertas obedientiae*.

Churchmen themselves have deplored the consequences of ecclesiastical prescription to art in the church. Not only, as Father Couturier regrets, have they caused the church to retreat from living art into one hundred years of mediocrity; they have cost it such great Catholic-born artists as Picasso, and have caused the abandonment of the very great body of free religious painting—the canvases of Georges Rouault are an instance—to a purely secular status. The traditional ecclesiastical Platonism, moreover, has been repeated and intensified by the new racist or etatist or proletarian Platonism of the Nazis and the Communists. What canon law forbids as modern and what Nazi statute condemns as *Kulturbolschewismus* and communist *ukase* denounces as bourgeois decadence, are the same thing. All presume that ethos can be made to measure by the command of authority, instead of being created in freedom.

In democratic societies censorship is environed by a great variety of checks and balances which may make it less direct, but not less arbitrary or less powerful. In the United States one of the most ominous concentrations of such arbitrary power is in the hands of the postmaster general and through him of such influences as he is sensitive to. A recent instance of its use is the strange post office tergiversation with the magazine *Esquire* and the surrealist journal *View*. The influence of pressure groups, ecclesiastical and other, on the post office and other police agencies of government is notorious, and ranges from organized aggression against speeches, books, and plays, to organized aggression against music. The composer Igor Stravinsky was a recent victim of one such aggression. He had performed at the Boston Symphony a brilliant arrangement he had himself composed of "The Star-Spangled Banner." There is a Massachusetts statute which penalizes any tampering with this anthem, no matter how much better it may be made, with imprisonment and fines. Stravinsky, being a famous composer, was only warned not to do it again.

IX

Now the power of censorship is inevitably power over communication. The anxious Jews of Amsterdam who excommunicated Spinoza first tried to silence the great philosopher with a bribe. They were quite willing that he should think what he chose as freely as he would; they could only not risk that he should say what he thought for others to hear. Ideas become powers only as they are communicated, not as they are expressed. No force on earth, not even the late Nazi and the Japanese, can prevent men from thinking as they will. Every idea, every image, begins as soliloquy and passes over into communication. The intent of censorship is to prevent soliloquy from becoming communication. Consequently in relation to his community, the artist is impotent unless his freedom of expression is supported by and prolonged into freedom of communication. Free trade in ideas is as indispensable to free art as free art is to cultural abundance. And these can neither be nor grow without free enterprise in communication. Here again, the safety lies in numbers. The greater the number and variety of independent newspapers, magazines, theatres, motion-picture producers, radio chains, art museums, orchestras, schools, and colleges, the more likely it is that, paraphrasing Mr. Justice Holmes, the artist can enrich the culture of his people by putting the power of his expression to the test of the competition of the markets. The economy of the market has, however, become inimical to competition. Industrial society adds to the censorship of church and state the censorship of monopolists of instruments of communication. A certain cartelization of communication is in process. The growth of great newspaper and magazine chains, the great radio networks, the motion-picture trusts, and the like, works unfriendly-wise

157

toward free communication. That which is communicated through these instruments is solely that which those who rule them choose to have communicated. If no artist has already expressed it, they command its expression from the stables of writers and painters and musicians whom they are able to keep on hire to serve them; and if the productions of their servants do not fit their purposes, they revise the work until it does; or, having paid for it and owning it, let it die unseen, unheard. The consequence is always a threat and ever more frequently a complete check to free communication with the result of first an inhibition and then an atrophy of artistic creation.

X

The creative spirit and the free trade in ideas are interdependent. The first without the second creates works without substance, repetitive, barren, and trivial like those of the medieval schools and the isolated island peoples of the South Seas. The second without the first comes to a quick end, for people do not trade in the same ideas, forms and goods and services, but in different ones. Novelty, variety, difference are the *sine qua non* of trade and the ground of abundance, whether spiritual or material, and freedom is the *fons et origo* of novelty, variety, and difference. If these are held by authoritarians to be a threat to the security of their monopolies, whether of things or thoughts, they are by the same token the safeguards of the freedom of free societies. Their symbol and concretion are, for the reasons we have reviewed, the freedom of the artist. The ethos of democracy needs a free art to express and to channel it, and free art needs the guarantees and protections of free society. President Roosevelt had said it, in his address at the opening of the Museum of Modern Art in New York:

The arts cannot thrive except where men are free to be themselves and to be in charge of the discipline of their own energies and ardors. The conditions for democracy and for art are one and the same. What we call liberty in politics results in freedom in the arts. . . . As in our democracy we enjoy the right to believe in different religious creeds or in none, so can American artists express themselves with complete freedom from the strictures of dead artistic tradition or political ideology. While American artists have discovered a new obligation to the society in which they live, they have no compulsion to be limited in method or manner of expression.

Of course, this is an overoptimistic statement, a declaration of principle and policy rather than a summary of the record. Especially doubtful, in view of that record, is the proposition "that what we call liberty in politics results in freedom in the arts." If freedom is that which we have here taken it to be, and if its career in the struggle for its existence is at all evidential, the truth is rather the converse: the civil liberties of men are initiated in the creative freedom of the artist. The latter is prior because it is primal; it is not freedom in the arts which results from democracy, but democracy which results from freedom in the arts. Those who remember the making of the Second French Republic remember a notable instance of this sequence. But it is true that once democratic society is established, the relationship becomes reciprocal; free art inspiring free society and free society safeguarding the liberty of art. Art can stay free however only in the degree that society affords the artist the security of a living as well as the liberty of a life, only as it keeps communication accessible and free. To withhold these is to suppress the liberty of art, and to suppress the liberty of art is like Herod's slaughter of the innocents—an attempt to kill off the alteration of the ideas, ideals, and ways and works of men at the source. The

159

liberty of the artist is the avatar of all the liberties of man. It subdues all discipline. It diversifies all doctrine. It never returns the same save as it brings the different. In the history of our culture, where the artists keep free no other sort or condition of man long remains bond.

Of Humanistic Sources

of Democracy

EACH OF the three words in the theme assigned to me—*humanistic, source, democracy*—is a word of many meanings. Each is extremely ambiguous. In usage, each is rendered specific and singular by the business and desire of the user. The critical term of the three is *source.* What do we mean by *source?* A consensus of the dictionaries would give us *spring,* a locus of origination or spontaneity. When this meaning is transposed into a universe of discourse called philosophy or metaphysics or theology, *source* becomes an alternate for *first cause.* The empirical equivalent for a *first cause,* least open to challenge, is probably the biologist's *gene.* So far as our knowledge presently goes, the gene is the one item in nature which consistently repeats itself and on occasion, alters itself. It not only reproduces itself in identical form, but varies spontaneously and then reproduces the variant together with its variations in identical form. The gene as cause appears to be a self-reproducing identity capable of change without self-liquidation. Although its alterings and mutations present themselves as discontinuous, they come as accretions to its own continuity, as accretions, that is, to a persistent identifiable nature and existence.

I

Now I shall take the term *source,* as applied to humanism, to mean a cause resembling a gene. I assume that what I am to do in this talk is to identify either a continuing or recurrent cause, called humanism, in the generation and upkeep of an effect, called democracy.

Inquiry into causes is today *par excellence* the enterprise of the scientist. Identifying causes is his vocation, even when the field is theology. The use of scientific method in theology and the treating of theology as a field for the scientific vocation are, I know, not exactly popular in certain circles, but they have their friends, who are a growing company. They are a growing company because the method of science has proved itself to be of all methods the most fruitful in that basic phase of the human enterprise which seeks to sort out and define those events which invariably bring about certain other events which someone feels to be of great moment for the life of man.

An undertaking beset with hazards and doubts in all the sciences, the designation of causes is particularly so in the social sciences, where the variables are countless and the constants are few, if not altogether lacking; and where a student may select any one or any group of the current components of an institution or an event, attribute to them causal efficacy, and support his attribution with rationalizations and statistical tables whose mathematics are infallible. This can be done even if the elected components are in fact not at all sources or agents; it can be done with the greatest of ease wherever the uses of things which are at once consequences and modifications of the natures of those things are treated as the origins, the springs whence their natures have drawn or draw their existence. For example, it is well known that many great and influential

162

democratic originals, such as Thomas Jefferson, made considerable use of certain classical writers whose productions are conventionally allocated to the humanities. But whether these humanities made a democrat of Jefferson and were causes of the beatitudes of democracy which we call the Declaration of Independence cannot be decided on the basis of use or purpose. It is no more likely that Jefferson, having studied the humanities, became a democrat, than that Jefferson, being a democrat, chose from the humanities those utterances which would nourish and sustain his democratic works and ways. But the disposition to call an event which preceded another event the cause of that which follows is inveterate, and the temptation to do so is particularly strong in history and the other social sciences, so that it is not hard to call certain of the humanities which figure in Jefferson's spiritual history causes of his democracy *post hoc propter hoc.* I shall try not to be led into this temptation, either with respect to Jefferson or with respect to any of the diverse sequences of humanistic and democratic ideas.

I shall also hope to by-pass a number of other temptations. One of these consists in declaring different meanings to be one and the same because they are communicated by means of a single term, word, or sign. It is as if oil and vinegar and water and wine and peroxide and quicksilver should be declared the same because they are carried in identical bottles. The identity of the vehicle contaminates the diversity of the passengers and their variety and multitude are masked by its unity. One of the most significant instances of such contamination of meanings by symbols which usage provide is of course the familiar word *God.* It is a word employed by Plato, by Cleanthes, by Plotinus, by St. Augustine, by St. Thomas, by Spinoza, by Jefferson, by Calvin, by Edward Scribner Ames, by Mordecai Kap-

163

lan, by William James, by Sitting Bull, by Adolph Hitler, and by countless other psychologists, metaphysicians, and theologians. However different the language of these men, the dictionaries make their words for God equal and interchangeable, and translate each as the alternate of any. But how can the men's meanings be made equal and interchangeable without terrible violence to the integrity of those separate meanings? Such violence can readily be done to the meanings of *humanism* and *democracy* when verbal illations mask fundamental divergences of intention. Such identifications are produced, as a rule, whenever we are passionately concerned with the survival and domination of one intention, regardless of the consequences to all others. For example, such a passionate concern is attributable to many who insist on deriving the democratic idea from Thomas Aquinas. As a matter of logic and history the derivation is, to say the least, highly debatable; as a postulate of passion it isn't debatable, nor is the passion debatable. Affirming itself, it involves either the ignoring or the overriding of that which is different from itself or the identification of the different with itself. At its most likely it confuses resemblance with sameness, analogy with identity.

This mode of mistakenly attributing causes is another one of the temptations into which the social scientist is all too often led. His sciences abound in analogical thinking, and a great deal of it is striking and some of it is fruitful. There is no need to quarrel with it. But there is great need to be extremely cautious about employing it as a method for bringing to light sources, causes, or agencies, be they enduring and supporting or transitory and lapsing. Transitory and lapsing causes occur in the social process at least as frequently as parents. Parents beget and get children, and not even the most intransigent theologian would hesitate to regard them as the sources or causes of at least the bodily being of their children. And so they are; they originate, they give rise to, and with this their parental efficacy consummates itself. It consists in a single act, largely contingent. It does not and cannot persist. After it has occurred parents are only the conditions and occasions of the being of their child, not its enduring and sustaining causes. Once a child is born its existence and survival are independent of its parentage. Its parentage—as of Jewish children in anti-Semitic societies—may render its existence precarious and its survival doubtful, or—as in all Nazidom—contribute causally to its torture and destruction. Once something has begun to exist, its survival and extinction are either functions of its own strengths and weaknesses or of the strength and weakness of the enduring source of which it is an overflow and which sustains it. If its source is transitory and lapses, then, be it a man-child, an idea, a natural object, or a human production, it survives or perishes as it goes and stops, on its own.

Beside these two meanings of the term *source* we must place another, which recurs frequently in certain types of scientific inquiry. This third meaning identifies source with *premise* or *ground*. When *source* is employed in this way, the connection between that which is spring and that which is flow is logical, not dynamic. Thus, if the relationship between humanism and democracy is considered dynamic, democracy will be an effect of humanism, not a conclusion from humanism; humanism will be a necessary antecedent of democracy, but democracy will not be a necessary consequence of humanism. If, on the other hand, the relationship between humanism and democracy be the relationship of a syllogistic ground or premise to a syllogistic conclusion, then humanism implies democracy and democracy is a necessary inference from humanism. To those who think of

165

the term *source* in this way, democracy can exist only if and
as humanism exists; the historic passage from humanism
to democracy is incidental, is only an explication in time of
an implication eternally present in the nature of human
events. Many writers treat the relation between humanism and democracy as if it were of this character. As I read
the record, the treatment is not an insight into the nature
of the facts but the operation of a desire to conform the
facts to a certain interest; it seems to me fundamentally
debatable.

II

So much, then, for the term *source*. Let us now discuss
the terms *humanism, democracy*. Their meanings, too, are
diverse and conflicting, and each is, especially in these
times of ours, subjected to too much variation to make it
possible to elicit, in the manner of a physicist or chemist
or mathematician, the quality of cause, agency, or ground
in their relations to one another. The most that I can
honestly do is to choose one or more of these meanings, review their sequence, their similarities, their divergences
with a view to discovering what is cause and what is effect,
and warn you that the choice cannot but express my own
social passion and personal interest. Other people make
other selections, as is their right. But mine is the only one
about which I can speak with any degree of certainty, and
over which I hold such authority as it is decent to hold.

Since the task is to discern the nature of the relation between humanism and democracy, it is proper to seek first
a meaning for democracy. The term appears early. Plato
used it, Aristotle used it, Jefferson used it, and spokesmen
of all sorts of interests and pretensions are using it today.
The multitude of meanings are not reconcilable. That
which I choose for discussion is Jefferson's. His meaning

of democracy is unique. Its coming into existence as a fighting faith for all mankind can be variously dated, but I accept a conventional date arbitrarily just as one accepts an individual's birthday arbitrarily; arbitrarily, because as is well known and well ignored, an individual is begotten and goes through a long and not unadventurous process of gestation and development before he is born. His birth is but a new turn, a happy or a tragic turn as you will, in a biography already launched; and if you wanted to extrapolate backward, you could set the birth of the individual at the beginning of the universe. This way of doing is not uncommon among philosophers of all sects, from theists and idealists to dialectical materialists and logical positivists.

Now the conventional birthday of democracy was July 4, 1776. On that day a conception was made flesh in an act, and the course of human events took a new turn. A war for independence and freedom was justified and its goals were defined by the signing of the document known as the Declaration of Independence, for the support of which the signers mutually pledged each other their lives, their fortunes, and their sacred honor. Seven propositions of this Declaration compose the unique beatitudes of the democratic faith of our times. Verse by verse, they read as follows:

We hold these truths to be self-evident [Jefferson had written "sacred and undeniable," but the phrase had been replaced with self-evident.]
that all men are created equal,
that they are endowed, by their Creator, with certain unalienable rights (Jefferson had written "inherent and unalienable," but the Congress struck out "inherent and" and stuck in "certain"),
that among these are life, liberty and the pursuit of happiness.

167

That to secure these rights governments are instituted among
men,

deriving their just powers from the consent of the governed,

that whenever any form of government becomes destructive
of these ends, it is the right of the people to alter or abolish it,
and to institute new government, laying its foundation on such
principles, and organizing its powers in such form, as to them
shall seem most likely to effect their safety and happiness.

This is the all of the modern democratic faith and a man
can learn it, as a certain gentile once wanted to learn Judaism, while standing on one leg. When, however, we come to
the business of interpreting and implementing the articles
of this faith in the works and ways of the daily life, the
case is different. A great deal of confusion obtains. One
such confusion turns upon the meanings which different
interpreters undertake to give to the term "equal" in the
proposition "that all men are created equal." To some it is
nonsense, a glittering generality flung obviously in the face
of all experience. To others it expresses a metaphysical
truth and is "self-evident" alone as such; namely, that the
manifest differences between men are but appearances,
unsubstantial and unimportant, that in truth and in reality
men are identical and not different, each and every one
being the same with each and every other and as interchangeable as machine parts.

The first interpretation, when brought to action, leads
to a struggle to perpetuate the modes of human association
which the Declaration challenged and denied; it leads to
asserting and preserving invidious distinctions; to dividing
the people as masters and servants on the basis of differences in faith, race, sex, birth, occupation, possessions, and
culture; to penalizing the different for being different by
shutting them into the servant class and keeping them
there.

168

The second interpretation brought to action leads to a struggle to bring out the hidden metaphysical equality or sameness, by demanding that those different in faith, race, sex, birth, occupation, possessions, and culture shall liquidate their differences and conform their being to some type or standard defined by power and commanded with authority. Many *soi-distant* "Americanization" movements have been enterprises of this kind, purporting to transform the different into the same. In the actualities of the daily life their methods and results have not been distinguishable from those of the interests which treat the idea that all men are created equal as a glittering generality. Both merely penalized the different for being different. Both made difference a ground of the invidious distinctions essential to setting up and maintaining a citizenship of the second class.

But it was precisely against this invidiousness, this penalization of the different that the Declaration set the nation's will. When it was framed, men and women everywhere in the world were being penalized for being what they were. Women, being female and not male, had no rights that their male relatives needed to respect; Catholics penalized Protestants and Protestants penalized Catholics and each other—all but the Quakers, who were penalized for being Quakers by all the other Christian denominations, while the Jews everywhere in the Christian world were penalized for not being Christians. Negroes were penalized for their color, poor men for their poverty, and men who worked with their hands, and were thus no gentlemen, for working with their hands. With the proposition "that all men are created equal," the Declaration nullified all that. The men who wrote and signed the Declaration and the men and women who fought and suffered and died for it did not intend by that proposition either to abol-

169

ish or to penalize differences. They intended to vindicate differences, to acknowledge, and to defend their *equal* right to life, liberty, and the pursuit of happiness. They affirmed the right to be different and the parity of the different as different. They did not look to any hidden metaphysical equality; they looked to the common, everyday experience that people who are different from each other can and do live together with each other on the basis that each has an equal title to the rights of life, liberty, and pursuit of happiness and that these rights are inherent and unalienable in each.

The Declarants were neither ignorant of nor ignored the historic and present fact that much of such living together consists in mutual alienations of life and liberty and happiness. They knew that the family, the field, the workshop, the school, the playground, the hall of government, the battlefield, all too often show themselves separately and together as very much like the jail and the gallows, techniques of such mutual alienations of these putative unalienable rights. But the Declarants never meant by "unalienable" that men and women did not kill and maim and frustrate each other, fence each other in and fend each other off. They meant "unalienable" to be a synonym for "inherent," for "constitutive." They meant that the nature of any and every human being, whatever his color, sex, race, faith, occupation, or social status, is constituted by these rights as a triangle is constituted by three sides and three angles; they meant that life, liberty, and the pursuit of happiness make up the substance of human nature, as the angles and sides of a triangle make up the being of the triangle; that hence, so long as a man is alive he will struggle to go on living, to be free, and to seek happiness; that this, his characteristic mode of being, may be attacked, may be mutilated, may be destroyed, but that he cannot behave otherwise than so. Alienation of these unalienable rights, then, is like cutting off a limb or a head, an attack on the inward human essence, not the withdrawal of something called a right that can be put on and put off like a garment or granted and withheld like a gift.

If there is any humanism in the Declaration, it is enfolded in this, its affirmation that rights are inherent and unalienable, that they constitute the nature of men, each different from the others and each equal with the others; that as such they are both the spring and the goal of human societies. The proposition, "to secure these rights governments are instituted among men" retains today much of the revolutionary intent it had when it was announced. For those who hold the powers of government, often even in democracies, reveal an inveterate propensity to regard these powers as those of a master, not of a servant, and to treat government as an autonomous end and not a means to other ends. The rationalizations of this propensity are many, but the most ancient and respectable is that which names God as the source and sanction of any power, good or evil. Kings and popes and nobles and clergy rule over the common man by divine right; their authority may not be challenged, nor their commandments disobeyed, because they speak in God's name and as his delegates on earth. When the Declaration was made, nearly all the political and ecclesiastical establishments of the world operated on a general assumption that men were made for governments, not governments for men, that men owe them obedience and service by God's will.

Against this prevailing assumption the Declaration set its principle "to secure these rights governments are instituted among men." It declared the inherent and unalienable rights of man to be the end, government only a means; it made the people the master, government the servant; it

171

made life, liberty and the pursuit of happiness the purpose, government an instrument to attain this purpose.

Moreover, by setting the origin of the just powers of government in the consent of the governed, the Declaration rejected the claims of divine sanction for the powers of all monarchs whether secular or ecclesiastical as false claims contrary to the truths about human nature as the Declaration affirms these truths. It implies that only just powers can hold the sanction of the consent of the governed, and that powers not so sanctioned, whatever may be claimed for them, are unjust. And all forms of government are, by implication, unjust when they become "destructive of these ends." Then the people have the right to treat them as they would treat any other agency or instrument which they have devised and used for the purposes of life, liberty, and happiness. They may enlarge, contract, or reshape their tools so as to make them fitter for the purposes they should serve. They may invent new tools and throw the others aside. There is no supernal authority, no infallible doctrine and discipline by which to judge the works of state or church or economic establishment or any organization of interest you will. Doctrine and discipline are agencies which serve, not masters that rule; their only measure is how well they serve to secure the equal rights of different people to life, liberty, and the pursuit of happiness.

III

Such, in sum, is the meaning which I find democracy to draw from the propositions of the Declaration of Independence. As I read the record, it involves a definite break with the entire tradition of the western world, including much of what is usually regarded as humanism. Before the in-

172

surgence of this idea of democracy neither the ancients nor the moderns failed to penalize this or that section of their own community and all the members of every other community for being different. Let alone the fact that chattel slavery was universal and endemic, the Greeks drew invidious distinctions between themselves and those whom they called barbarians; the Jews between themselves and the Gentiles; the Romans between themselves and their subject peoples, the Christians between themselves and the Jews, the heretics and the infidels. In each case the different must not be equal but subordinate, second-rate, worthy only of subject status and servile occupation. Alike the pagan and the Judeo-Christian tradition affirmed some sort of supernatural sanction for their discriminations against other human beings. John Calvin brought this sanction to the ultimate height of metaphysical authority. He made a dogma of the proposition that, as Jefferson wrote in 1822 to Benjamin Waterhouse, "God, from the beginning, elected certain individuals to be saved, and certain others to be damned; and that no crimes of the former can damn them; no virtues of the latter save."

The attitude which this consummates is a component of the Greek view of life no less than of the Jewish, but the irony of history made it with the Jews an automatic compensation for their frustrations as a people. It is to them that the tradition attributes, not wrongly, the pretension of being *the chosen people*. Similar pretensions were and are operative among all the peoples of the world, but their expressions have not received equal importance. The Hellenes were not less elect to Plato and Aristotle than the Hebrews were to their prophets and rabbis, but the pagans did not erect this sentiment into a dogma of religion whence they might draw consolation and reassurance. The Jews did. Their God was God omnipotent and just, yet he was capable of playing favorites and choosing out of the infinite multitude of his creatures one group to be his particular people and he to be their particular God, without, however, any fundamental detriment to other peoples, who were also declared to be God's creatures and care. If I understand the prophetic and Judaist view correctly, it was more psychological than logical. The election of Israel did not mean the rejection of the other nations; it meant not that the nations were rejected but only that Israel was preferred. The Christian employment of this dogma of reassurance and consolation carries its logic to the limit. Christian dogma changes the status of the Jews from that of the chosen people to that of the rejected people. According to it, just and omnipotent God chooses only those human beings who believe on the Christ and rejects and condemns to eternal damnation those who do not believe on the Christ. Calvin modified this classical view by adding that our finite minds cannot know whom, in the Christ, infinite God's omniscience and omnipotence has elected and whom rejected.

But whether we think of divine election after the manner of the Jews or after the manner of the Christians, we see the dogma as exercising a dominating influence in Judeo-Christian culture. We see it as a means of making and supporting invidious distinctions between man and man, as a rule for penalizing the different because it is different. In the climate of opinion where this dogma figures, equality is the synonym for similarity or identity; difference is condemned and rejected. Although holders of this dogma have recently discoursed eloquently and at length about "the infinite value of the human personality," they have not really meant any and every personality, with all its differences on its head. They have really meant personality that agrees or that is persuaded or that is tortured into

174

agreeing, and is thus become a member of God's elect who alone can be infinitely valuable; the otherwise-minded personality, being God's reject, is punished for its difference by being only infinitely valueless and damned.

But this is precisely what democracy negates. Democracy sanctions and encourages differences and confirms the equal right of each and all to life, liberty, and the pursuit of happiness. It alone affirms, without any fear of challenge or contradiction, "the infinite value of human personality." The practical working of its concept of equality may be best illustrated from the attitudes, opinions, and conduct of Thomas Jefferson, foremost of the builders of democracy into the works and ways of the American people. I say foremost because Jefferson was not only the author of the Declaration of Independence and the creator of the Bill of Rights; he was the leader in the enactment of these ideals into law in his own state of Virginia, by securing the abolition of entail and primogeniture, the disestablishment of churches, the promulgation of the world-famous bill for establishing religious freedom, and the bill for public education. As ambassador to France, as Washington's Secretary of State, as Vice-President under John Adams, as President for two terms, and as guide, philosopher, and friend of his disciples James Madison and James Monroe, he labored for a longer period than any other single personality in power toward shaping the political, the religious, the economic, the educational, and the cultural life of the United States at home and their foreign relations abroad toward the ways of the Declaration of Independence. In the domain of religion, for example, he sought the definition by law that churches are voluntary societies to which no man is bound by nature. "No man," he wrote in his "Notes on Virginia," "has power to let another prescribe his faith. Faith is not faith without belief." He held that no

church can claim jurisdiction over any other nor be forced
to pay for the upkeep of any other, that membership in a
church cannot be a condition prior to receiving civil rights
or a basis of withholding or withdrawing civil rights. The
value of a religion, he contended, is to be judged neither by
the origins claimed for it nor the powers it pretended to;
the value of a religion was to be judged by its consequences
to the liberties and happiness of men. Writing in 1803 to
Dr. Benjamin Rush, he called attention with approval to a
vote of the Pennsylvania legislature rejecting a proposal to
make belief in God a necessary qualification for public
office, "although there was not a single atheist among the
voters." Such a law would violate democracy by penalizing
citizens for not sharing the beliefs of the majority. He opposed successfully a ministerial undertaking to get the
phrase, "Jesus Christ, author of our holy religion," inserted
in the Virginia Statute of Religious Liberty—this, not because he failed to appreciate Jesus, but because it would
violate the very idea of the Statute.

Jefferson's appreciation of Jesus was singular and un-
paralleled: its consequence is what is called the Jefferson
Bible, which it would repay you and all Americans to study.
This Bible is a democrat's re-creation of "the life and morals
of Jesus of Nazareth," and cannot be correctly understood
except in the frame of reference of democracy. Its author
constructed it by taking together the Greek, Latin, French,
and English versions of the gospels, and the gospels only.
He cut parallel passages from each, in order to compare
them for agreements and differences, and he pasted them
accordingly in his notebook. The result was a document
which he called the philosophy of Jesus of Nazareth. What
emerges as important in this document is not what is regarded as important in Christian dogma. Jefferson lays no
emphasis on the death and resurrection of Jesus; he lays

176

all his emphasis on the social teachings of Jesus. And significantly, he brings these teachings together with certain of the teachings of Epicurus. Rejecting all but the words of Jesus that he believes to be authentic, he writes to John Adams, "I am a real Christian . . . a disciple of the doctrines of Jesus." Elsewhere he speaks of himself as an Epicurean and sees only harmony in the real Christian and Epicurean faiths. His contemporaries, all the clergy and the Federalist laymen, denounced his views of Jesus as blasphemous and atheistic. But they were views alone consistent with the propositions of the Declaration of Independence, views which enabled him to contribute with equal generosity to the Episcopal and Presbyterian churches of Charlottesville, both bitterly inimical to him, and to an enterprise for the purchase and free distribution of Bibles. They were views which, though he held a low opinion of Judaism, enabled him to write to Mordecai Noah: "Your sect by sufferings has furnished a remarkable proof of the universal spirit of religious intolerance inherent in every sect, disclaimed by all when feeble, and practiced by all when in power. Our laws have applied the only antidote to this view, protecting our religious, as they do our civil rights, by putting all on an equal footing. . . . It is to be hoped that individual dispositions will at length mold themselves on the model of the law, and consider the model bases, on which all religions rest, as the rallying point which unites them in a common interest."

This rallying point was to Jefferson the unalienable right to be different. To be different, therefore to doubt, to inquire, to study, and compare alternatives, a right no less unalienable to minorities than to majorities, also when a minority consists of one person only! Jefferson's deepest commitment was to the "illimitable freedom of the human mind to explore and expose every subject susceptible of its

177

contemplation!" He had sworn, he once declared, "upon the altar of God, hostility to every form of tyranny over the mind of man." Set this Jeffersonian conception of human relations beside that of an official of the city of Boston, commenting upon assaults made against Jews and Negroes in that sometime Athens of America. Said the official: "Democracy means majority rule, and Jews and Negroes are in the minority." The implication is that minorities have no rights that majorities need respect. A completer contravention of the democratic idea and the Jeffersonian faith could hardly have been expressed by a public official, nor an attitude more consistent with the tradition of privilege and authority.

The full, practical meaning of the democratic faith as a program of conduct is exemplified by nothing so much as its repudiation of slavery. Neither the classical world nor the Judeo-Christian ages of faith in fact rejected slavery. There were certain Stoic expressions against it, but no efficacious overt action. Thomas Aquinas, currently a much-cited authority in justification of democracy, was no more opposed to slavery than Aristotle or Luther or Calvin; the enslavement of the different was a testimony to the rightness and power of the elect. True, the history of the predemocratic world records many slave and serf uprisings—whether in Greece or Rome or Northern Europe or the Americas—uprisings in which the slaves fought for their own freedom; it does not record a single instance of free men fighting for the liberation of slaves. This does not occur until the democratic revolution. Jefferson had written a denunciation of slavery into the Declaration of Independence that powerful interests in the Continental Congress erased; and the same interests succeeded in writing safeguards of property in human beings into the Constitution. But there was not room in the same nation for both democ-

178

racy and slavery. From democracy's first day free men waged a war against slavery by tongue and pen, by stratagem and force. The war finally became a great civil war in which free men staked their all to set slaves free, and, having done so, wrote their victory into the fundamental law of the land, as one more step toward the conversion of the ideals of the Declaration of Independence into realities of the American way of life.

IV

Now, given this meaning for *democracy*, what has humanism contributed to it? Replies to this question will depend, obviously, on which of the many meanings of *humanism* one chooses to consider among the sources of democracy. Current discussion gives the conventional meaning a factitious potency. The conventional meaning is the academic meaning. It designates as humanism a concern with the humanities and the humanities as the secular literature, and sometimes the graphic and plastic arts of the "pagan" Greeks and Romans. This literature is *classical*. It is written in ancient Greek and Latin.[1] It bulks large among

---

[1] Jefferson himself had a humanistic education in this sense. His regard for the classics was such that he made them the core of the curriculum that he proposed for the students of his University of Virginia. In view of these facts, it is worth while putting into the record his opinion of the relation of the Greeks and Romans to democracy. I quote from two letters, one written in 1816 to I. H. Tiffany about the Greeks in the time of Aristotle; the other in 1819 to John Adams about the Romans:

To Tiffany Jefferson wrote:

"But so different was the style of society then and with those people, from what it is now with us, that I think little edification can be obtained from their writings on the subject of government. They had just ideas of the value of personal liberty, but none at all of the structure of government best calculated to preserve it. They knew no medium between a democracy . . . and an abandonment of themselves to an aristocracy or a tyranny independent of the people. It seems not to have occurred to them

lists of "hundred best books," which as a rule do not include anything written in Hebrew. The emphasis falls on its being secular. Thereby it is opposed to the Greek and Latin religious texts of our Judeo-Christian cults. Humanism began as a cultivation of those works of pagan man in preference to works produced by nonpagan men as glosses upon the revelations of Judeo-Christian God. It set those humanities against that divinity. It made secular society the peer and better than the peer of churchly. It exalted this-worldliness over other-worldliness, preferring the discourse of human reason to ukase concerning superhuman salvation. By and large, it was anticlerical, even in the church itself. Very many of the early humanists were ordained priests or

---

that where the citizens cannot meet and transact their business in person, they alone have the right to choose the agents who shall transact it, and that in this way a republican, or popular government, of the second grade of parity, may be exercised over any extent of country.

"The full experiment of government democratical, but representative, was and still is reserved for us. . . . The introduction of this new principle of representative democracy has rendered useless almost everything written before on the structure of government; and in a great measure, relieves our regret, if the political writings of Aristotle, or of any other ancient, have been lost."

To Adams Jefferson wrote:

"And if Caesar had been as virtuous as he was daring and sagacious, what could he, even in the plenitude of his usurped power, have done to lead his fellow citizens into good government? I do not say to *restore it*, because they never had it, from the rape of the Sabines to the ravages of the Caesars. . . . But steeped in corruption, vice and venality, as the whole nation was . . . what could even Cicero, Cato, Brutus have done, had it been referred to them to establish good government for their country They had no ideas of government themselves, but of their degenerate Senate, nor the people of liberty, but of the factious opposition of their Tribunes. They had afterwards their Tituses, their Trajans, and Antoninuses, who had the will to make them happy, and the power to mould their government into a good and permanent form. But it would seem as if they could not see their way clearly to do it. No government can continue good, but under the control of the people; and their people were so demoralized and depraved, as to be incapable of exercising a wholesome control."

monks. They were secretaries, librarians, prelates, popes. Others were officials, merchants, courtiers, princes. Their minds were first allured, then liberated by the alternatives to the authoritarian tradition which they encountered in the undogmatic thinking, varied contents, and perfect expression of such writers as Cicero, as Tacitus, as Ovid or Pliny or Varro, as Quintilian, as Plato, as Aristotle, whom they had come to read at first hand at last.

As for the most part, the clergy were the literati, the making of humanism was first a churchly event. Petrarch was a churchman, but like so many of his colleagues, he was a churchman in the same way as a physician is a physician who doesn't need to practice medicine for a living and spends his days painting pictures. The liberation and delight which the humanities brought clerics like Petrarch in the course of time carried the classical writers into the fanes, and made of them themes of disputation in the academic halls. To be a grammarian was for a time as exciting a vocation as to be an admiral of the ocean sea. It was not long before the humanists' eagerness regarding the humanities reached out to the originals of divinity. They dared to read the Scriptures in Hebrew and in Greek.

That which the humanists found in the Scriptures of the original tongues was not what authority had drawn from them. An impulse which had first been simple curiosity developed quickly into free inquiry challenging authority. The perusal of the sources at first hand revealed difference and variation in the sources themselves. The discovery of difference and variation led automatically to comparison, and then to the exaltation of the free movements of reason over the conformities of faith. These free movements created in the course of time what is today known as higher criticism. Its technique consisted in the direct observation, the watchful analysis, the careful comparisons and reorderings, the continuous over-all scrutiny which pertain to the methods of science.

The classical instance of a humanist according to this meaning of humanism is, of course, Erasmus. His *In Praise of Folly* is a judgment upon all users of authority of his day—the soldiers, the priests, the philosophers, the rhetoricians, the pedants, the landlords. His sense of the humanities makes him one of the great ironists of divinity, whose popes he regards as tyrants of the City of the World rather than servants of the City of God, whose friars sell salvation in the market place, whose scholastics find the choice between killing a thousand men and mending a beggar's shoe on Sunday a vital option and who are so learned that the apostles couldn't understand them, as they argue of how one body occupies two places, heaven and the cross, the right hand of God the Father and the consecrated wafer, and as they expound that Mary escaped Adam's sin. Erasmus not only read the New Testament in Greek; he undertook to translate it for the uses of the common people. To make his translation which, in 1516, he dedicated to Leo X, the most accurate in his power, he collated the best available manuscripts, comparing them verse for verse and chapter for chapter, recognizing inconsistencies, seeking the true version instead of the authorized one. Willy-nilly he found himself raising questions concerning the Epistle to the Hebrews, the Epistle of James, the Book of Revelation, the second and sixth chapters of John, the second of Peter, and so on. His concern was, like Jefferson's, the philosophy of Jesus. He prized the spirit, which is without price, more highly than the relics whose magic uses brought good prices. That which defined Erasmus as a humanist as distinguished from the champions of divinity was not merely his delighted knowledge of the classics. It was his method of treating differences with respect. It was his

182

readiness to accept the so-called unauthoritative on the same level as the authorized, to treat authority as a claim only that must make good by merit and not by rule, to exalt free inquiry, and to cultivate the toleration which such inquiry postulates. Thereby he gave Martin Luther sufficient cause to call him the "greatest enemy of Christ" and to proclaim that whoever crushed Erasmus would crush a bug that would stink even more when dead than when alive. Thus he gave the conformist churchmen sufficient cause to brand him as a heretic and to place all his works on the Index.

This sort of humanism is the antithesis of another kind which has had a certain vogue in the academic arcana of our time. Why its protagonists call it humanism has never been clear to me. I presume that they do so because their central concern continues to be the humaner letters of Greece and Rome which excited and liberated the humanists of the Renascence; that they disregard the Hebraic originals of our Judeo-Christian tradition, and fix their attention on Plato and pre-Christian platonism, and to a lesser degree on Aristotle. Their spokesmen in the United States have been the late Messrs. Paul Elmer More and Irving Babbitt. Mr. T. S. Eliot is a perverse half-English variant, and I do not doubt that many would associate with him our charming and eloquent French colleague M. Jacques Maritain. Although they call themselves humanists, their preoccupation is not, however, man nor the humanities, but God as conceived and defined by certain classical writers of whom the foremost is Plato. Their method, far from being that of the sciences of our day, is not even the over-all scrutiny, the careful observation, the free inquiry of Erasmus. Their method is authoritarian and dialectical. To them man's nature is dual and not one. It has a superior and an inferior part, a soul and a body, and

183

the body is all animal impulse and unchecked desires, while the soul is a unitary principle of human nature inwardly harmonious to, if not a derivative of, the universal and eternal being of God. Over against the multiplicity, the variety, the this-worldiness, of the modern sciences of man, these *soi-disant* humanists set a hidden single, indivisible eternal, universal human nature, which acts as an inner check on the phenomenal multiplicity and variety and holds them together and directs their ways by its infallible force.

Professor Werner Jaeger has written an illuminating and very sympathetic interpretation of the original of this species of humanism as it took form in the dialogues of Plato, with their antidemocratism, their racialism, their doctrine and discipline of authority, stated firmly but somewhat gently in the *Republic*, fiercely in the *Laws*, drawn from the "divine order." This has recently been published in English translation as volumes II and III of *Paideia, the Ideals of Greek Culture*. They bring to us the authentic root of what M. Jacques Maritain opts to call "theocentric humanism." And no democrat could take exception to it, if only it didn't, in Plato, explicitly condemn and excommunicate democracy; if only it didn't serve, after Plato, as a sanction for all the ways of penalizing the different of which democracy is the rejection. Not alone are the great religions of the world different from each other in countless specific ways, but each great religion is diversified into denominations, sects, and cults, everyone with its own characteristic singularity of imagining God and what he requires of man. There is the God of the theists and the God of the deists; there are the Gods of the polytheists and the God of the pantheists. There is one God who is all reason, another who is all love, another who is all will. There is a God who is all spirit and a God who is no less body than spirit. The *theos* of the theocentric humanists differs from sect to sect and man to man and land to land. The center of his humanism is not one but many.

If our theocentric humanist accepts this fact, if he does not presume to excommunicate all other centers but his own as false and evil; if he does not undertake to compel other men to center on his one as *the* One, laying upon them all the penalties of the record should they refuse; if he acknowledges the equal right of different men to think their Gods in such a manner as shall to each seem best for enhancing his life, liberty, and pursuit of happiness, then his center is in fact not God but men. Then the *theos* is not invoked as the justification of coercion and tyranny, but becomes the agency "to secure these rights"; then the human being is set free by means of the *theos*. Then the idea or image or being of God is taken honestly and openly for that which in the history of civilization it actually is— a function of mankind's struggles for life, liberty, and happiness. The God upon whom a man centers becomes then like the wife of his bosom, the hearth of a home of his own, instead of the noble lady whose beauty and virtue it is his knightly mission to compel other men to acknowledge by the force of his infallible sword. The fascist's State, the Nazi's race, the Japanese's goddess, the Communist's dialectic of matter cannot offer themselves as rivals and substitutes of this God. He is plural, not singular; multitudinous, not totalitarian; man is the measure of him, not he the measure of man. He is the God of the tradition of Protagoras, not the God of the tradition of Plato. He is the figure of a humanism which stems from the *humanitas* that, during the second century before the Christian era, came to existence among certain Romans of sensibility and sense after their minds had been awakened and their hearts opened by the impact of the philosophy of Epicurus, with

185

its social detachment, its charity, and its intellectual freedom. *Humanitas* was the humanism of the Scipionic circle.
It comes—altogether accidentally, perhaps—to its high
place of expression in a comedy by a member of that circle,
the African Terence, who had been a slave and had been
manumitted. In this play, based on one of Menander's
(*Heauton Timoroumenos*), trivial in plot, for the most part
trivial in utterance, a character pronounces lines that have
become part of the wisdom of aspiration of our western
world. They are: *Homo sum, humani nihil a me alienum
puto.*

Legend has it that the audience which first heard this line
rose in tumultuous applause. The line had stopped the
show. But its meaning, which has haunted the hearts of men
ever since, did not get beyond the show until the democratic revolution, nor lightly, nor without blood and sweat
and tears since. This meaning is at the center of still another
conception of humanism which, being a consequence and
function of democracy, knowingly prefers among the
thinkers of classical antiquity Protagoras, the plebeian, to
Plato, the aristocrat. This humanism is sometimes identified
with the pragmatism of William James. Its spokesman is
the late F. C. S. Schiller, one of William James's foremost
and most original disciples. In his *Plato or Protagoras,* Schiller throws into a fresh perspective the debate between the
former Asiatic self-taught porter and inventor, friend of
Pericles and Euripides, bait of Aristophanes, and the
Athenian nobleman. The works of Protagoras are lost to us.
Some were burned by the Athenians; others have perished.
What remains are a few sentences which indicate why.
They point to a man-centered humanism, to *humanitas.*
"Man," wrote Protagoras, "is the measure of all things, of
things that are, that they are, of things that are not, that
they are not." The point of importance is that man is the

186

measure, not the creator. Whatever his philosophy, he has to take things as experience brings them to him, and he has to value them in terms of their bearing on his life and liberty and pursuit of happiness. Before he can say that this does exist, or that that does not exist, he must have some impression, some idea, of this and that. They must be present somehow, to be declared nonexistent, even as they must be present, somehow, to be declared existent. The presence must make itself felt, and as felt, may be measured. This measurement is a human art; it is the all of the method and the content of science; the spring of the body of knowledge. Considering the Gods as objects of measurement, Protagoras declares in another fragment, "with regard to the Gods, I cannot feel sure that they are or they are not, nor what they are like in figure. For there are many things that hinder sure knowledge; the obscurity of the subject, and the shortness of human life."

These are presumably passages from Protagoras' book *On Truth.* He had read from it in the house of Euripides to a company of free minds of the Greek enlightment. To some theocentric humanist there present it must have been blasphemy. Protagoras was denounced and condemned to death. He fled Athens, but the book was burned.

As I read the record, an ultimate statement of this meaning of humanism is to be found in the Book of Job, which is itself an assimilation of Greek form to Hebraic insight. There is a familiar, oft-repeated English verse, "Though he slay me will I trust in him." The Hebrew original, correctly translated, reads: "Behold, he will slay me; I shall not survive; nevertheless will I maintain my ways before him." Another verse declares: "Mine integrity hold I fast and will not let it go; my heart shall not reproach me so long as I live." These are words which the author puts in the mouth of Job in reply to his theocentric comforters,

187

who argue that since his torture must be from God, he can be relieved of it only if he looks upon himself as God looks upon him, admits his sin, and repents. But Job will not repudiate his human dignity. He contends for the integrity of his human essence even against the inscrutable absoluteness of omnipotent God. Between him and that God there is no common measure, for what measure has man save his human passions and human values, and how can these be applied to omnipotence and omniscience without limiting and belittling it? In consequence, Job, the symbol of all men, must stand up on his own feet alone, working out his destiny by his own measure, recognizing that a just and omnipotent God cannot indulge in a chosen people, cannot elect a favorite, but must maintain all his creatures with an equal providence, thus vindicating the right of each to his different integrity. For the claimant to election by omnipotence also claims the rule of omnipotence; it becomes a pretension to mastery over all mankind and thus a threat of war and slavery to the different, and ultimately of disaster to the pretender himself, be it a single person, a state, or a church.

Humanism in this meaning has a certain kinship with democracy. But it was elicited from the Book of Job after the democratic revolution. Before that revolution Job was treated as a vindication and proof of the authoritarian ways of an authoritarian God.

V

I think we may now come to some conclusion concerning humanistic sources of democracy. Certain humanisms provide obvious analogies with democracy; others, no matter what is claimed for them nor who claims it, are altogether incommensurable. Analogic humanisms are such because of certain techniques or attitudes or processes which occur also in the ways of democracy. But the authentic humanists of history to whom those pertained, such as Erasmus, had no inkling of modern democracy and in all likelihood would have been shocked by it. Their humanism was not a source of democracy because their end, their goal, their stopping-place, was this humanism, not democracy. Again, it was not a source because although democracy follows, it does not follow from this humanism. The latter is chronologically prior; only, however, in so far as certain of its aspects are a dynamic common to both itself and democracy, may it be designated as a source. Those aspects, we have seen, are not the intellectual or aesthetic content of this humanism; they are the methods of the humanists, in the degree that they consist in observation, free inquiry, unrelaxing scrutiny of thoughts and things. The humanism which works by the methods of authority, which sets dogma above observation, rationalization above reason, and belief and obedience above scrutiny and free choice cannot be said to contribute anything to democracy.

Lastly, there is also a humanism which may be taken as a synonym for democracy. But it would be as correct to hold that that democracy is the source of this humanism as that this humanism is a source of democracy. For democracy is chronologically prior to this humanism. Even though it does employ Protagoras and Terence to support its vision, it comes to expression in a social atmosphere, in a climate of culture, where the propositions of the Declaration of Independence are the gradients for human relations and the methods of science for human discourse. This humanism, hence, is pluralistic, empirical, and libertarian. Its spokesmen acknowledge, respect, and endeavor sympathetically to understand differences and the co-operation of differences. They hold with William James in his *Will to Believe:*

"No one of us ought to issue vetoes to the other, nor should we bandy words of abuse. We ought, on the contrary, delicately and profoundly to respect one another's mental freedom." Instead of demanding or exacting conformity, they endeavor to live and let live, to live and help live. God, some of them argue, is, on the record, either a name for companies of many divine beings struggling for survival as human beings struggle, and forming their association with other species, not the human only, according to its role in this survival; or else God is a name for an all-powerful entity, differently imagined by different men, that brings forth impartially all the infinite diversities of experience, not men only, nor what men find good and what men find evil; and that just as impartially sustains and destroys them all. God so conceived, these humanists hold, cannot favor man over any other species; nor any race or cult of man over any other; nor any human doctrine and discipline over any other. All maintain themselves or perish, under such a God, not by favor, but by their own dispositions and abilities. According to these humanists each form of existence, has, under such a God, its own different type of life, liberty, and happiness; each has an equal right with every other to achieve its type. Among men, each comes together with others to form societies—churches, states, economies, civilizations—because by these means each can "secure these rights" more aptly, more abundantly, than he could alone. The means become the One, generated by the Many. Institutions and governments are at their best when their oneness is thought of and treated not as organism but as organization, when they express not unity but union, when they consist not in integration but orchestration, when they are modes of the free association of the different—organizations of liberty whose just powers are the hearts and the heads of all the human beings whose organizations they are.

There may be other, and as apt, orchestrations of humanism with democracy. If there are, I must regretfully declare that I have missed them. But I do not think there are; for when humanism is taken thus humanly, democracy is humanism, humanism is democracy.

Freedom in the Factory

I

NO CONTEMPORARY, talking about freedom, finds it easy to put into words a clear and distinct notion of what he means. The traditional obscurities are made darker than ever by the complications which both science and industry have added to our ways of living and our ways of thinking. By comparison, freedom was, to the preindustrial world a notion simple indeed. It is this notion, in its religious simplicity, which is still used in the law, where it finds asylum from the ruins of a theology that passes. Men, the law presumes and the lawyers argue and the judges decide, choose their actions and are responsible for them. Men's actions are consequences of their choices between right and wrong. They know the difference and merit the results. Of course, there are times when men do not know the difference; and there are times when their choosing is coerced. In the first instance, they are not quite human; in the second, they have not really themselves made the choice. They cannot be held responsible because they had not in fact been free. Such cases are, however, exceptional.

Now, what the law holds to be the exception, science declares to be the rule. What the law holds to be the rule, science declares never happens. Science requires that we shall look beyond the individual man, that we shall see him, not isolated, but in the light of what goes on before him and around him. If we do that, we recognize that he is nothing by himself, that what he does is only the last link, the present effect, in an endless chain of causation, which was of infinite power before he was born and will not diminish when he dies.

Industry, again, has taken the free craftsman and set him down in front of a machine to whose motion he is tied. It has changed him from a general worker to a specialized operative in a would-be continuous and even process of making, selling, consuming, and making again. Into this process the operative is fitted like a cog to another cog on wheels turning endlessly round; over his movements in the rotation he has no more control than have the hands of a clock over their movements upon its face. Save when he is hired and fired, or bawled out for such a slip as any wearing machine part might make, he is not a person with a proper name, but a hand in the shop, a numbered machine part, making movements he does not initiate, producing results he does not intend and owns no part in. He is just another mechanical link in the endless chain of equivalent causes and effects.

As special interest directs or occasion renders desirable, every contemporary is treated, now according to one of these views of his nature, now according to the other. The trend of what is known as humanitarianism has been to conceive personality under the aspect of scientific determinism and mechanical industry. Ideals of reform in industry, in penology, in the very structure of civilization as such are postulated upon the rejection of the traditional view that an individual is a free personal will continually choosing between alternatives, and responsible for his choices.

II

But if the freely choosing will is denied, what other thing in life can freedom mean? What is affirmed by the expression *free individual?*

The answer, at once classic and traditional, harks back to the structure and movement of the clock. The clock began with modern science and is one of the first machines of modern industry. Its dominion is coextensive with the modern world, and it might in fact be said that by its power has the modern world been made. Industrial man lives entirely under its rule. Its inward articulation and outer autonomy, its precise and measured self-repetitive beat, all so neat, so compact, so self-contained and self-sufficient, have fascinated and held the imagination since Newton's day. Consider. The clock is wound up and runs down. Its wheels within wheels are cogged, and every cog is formed for its preordained push and pull against preordained mates. All cogs fit; there is a place for each and each is in its place. The spring is wound, the cogs impinge, the wheels turn, the clock ticks, the hands go round. The clock is going. It goes so long as nothing intervenes to clog the wheels. Should something clog them, the clock must stop. And never can this something come from within the clock. It is an intrusion from without. Uninvaded, the clock wound up runs down. The movement, inevitable, predetermined, as it is, is yet free.

A like freedom is sometimes presumed to pertain to the human personality, body and soul together. The machinery of muscles and nerves and glands is cogged and fitted so that it moves the body; the passions and purposes of character are integrated and drive the personality, from birth to death. Our life is but the running down of a human clock, wound up with birth and unwound at death. Much that is called modern in psychology—behaviorism, for example, or psychoanalysis—employs assumptions concerning the personality and character of men which rest upon the unremembered but active analogy with the clock. Indeed, theology also exhibits such assumptions, for both deists

194

and pantheists see God as ultimately nothing more than such a living clock, self-winding and self-wound and going from eternity. His freedom is his self-determination. As he has no environment, nothing can enter from without to clog his works, and so he is able according to the laws of his own nature to move in his mysterious ways his wonders to perform, from everlasting unto everlasting. Mankind, unluckily, are creatures in an environment, subject to the impact and arrest and distortion of its forces. Soon or late, their works get clogged. The environment imposes adjustments and readjustments altering, not only the running of the human machine, but its shape, its size, its outward form, and inward goal.

Thus, the determinism intrinsic to the divine nature is a far, far simpler one than that which rules the children of man. The play of cause and effect in human nature is far more complicated and indiscernible than the uncomplicated, logical self-determination wherein the theologians define the unchanging nature of God. In human life there is give and take between uncounted forces that the sciences of man and of nature endeavor to discern, to identify, and to measure. So doing, they treat the conduct of men as a play of wish-gratifying and pain-avoiding mechanisms in action amid a diversified environment in which both pains and satisfactions may be encountered indifferently. Modernly, this treatment is called by the new and imposing names of the social sciences. But in its essence it is an ancient—a classical—procedure. It involved, from the very beginning, the recognition that freedom cannot be merely the unobstructed running-down of what had been wound-up; that it must be an aspect of the process of attaining good and avoiding evil in a habitation which was not made to be man's home, which is merely a place where man happened and grew and struggles to survive. How can he succeed, if not by desiring only that which he can attain, by accepting all that he cannot avoid? So, he ceases to be at war with the conditions of his existence. He acknowledges and accepts them, and in accepting them he acquiesces in his own being.

Such acquiescence is usually called spiritual. It defines a way of life which in various forms is recommended by the religions of the world. The man who comes to his freedom through such acquiescence is usually a religious man. He has given up worldly things and his own will. He has become ascetic. He has said to the power not himself: "Thy will, not mine, be done." His language may have been that of the Stoic, the Epicurean, the Buddhist, the Christian, the Mohammedan. But whatever his language, its meaning is that his freedom is self-surrender, nonresistance and acquiescence, that he wins it by ceasing to struggle for his life, by losing it and its purposes in the life and the purposes of God, or in the processes and laws of nature.

Managements commonly preach a similar sinking of the worker's personality in the industry or business they manage. Sometimes their preaching is adopted as the worker's practice but rarely for long. With the best will, employees are soon disillusioned about the freedom which comes through identifying themselves thus with their jobs. Their position and its consequences are not the same as those of the religious and the philosophical. The latter do not make this identification under blind submission to authority, on sheer faith. In them it is the consequence of an experience of illumination, the climax of a religious and philosophical insight. When saint or sage declares "Thy will, not mine, be done," he does so because he feels he has certain and true knowledge of what this will is, and what it is after. He is not a soldier obeying a command given in a battle of whose strategy he is unaware and in whose tactics he is a mere pawn. He feels himself rather to be a comrade as well as a soldier of the lord, assenting to and thereby sharing in the divine plan. This voluntary assent and participation constitute his freedom.

Of course this freedom has its paradoxes. If a train carries you off when you had not wanted to ride on it, riding willingly because ride you must may relieve you from the anxiety and strain which resistance would involve, but it does not cease to be true that you have other wishes and that you would have gone elsewhere if you could. So long as you are you, these other wishes remain ineluctably and forever unidentifiable with the want and will you accept and acquiesce in. Short of suicide, complete identification, utter acquiescence, cannot occur. You cannot both be something in and for yourself and lost in and for another, be that other God or Nature. So long as you retain any identity whatsoever you do not altogether submit. "Thy will, not mine, be done" implies as a proviso, "so far as it is compatible with the survival of my individuality and the upkeep of what is most essential to my being."

III

How spontaneous and ineluctable this reservation is can be recognized by anyone who cares to inspect the actualities of freedom in the common life. Who are the people and what are they, other than the saints and sages, whom we look upon as free or who look upon themselves as free? They are, in the first instance, people not under the duress of certain types of burden, nor tethered to the serving of certain needs. The *free souls*, the men and women who have their freedom live in an elemental and definite security. They enjoy a basic social safety which the unfree lack. In the setting of this safety they move and act freely. They

197

pursue their desires and are not afraid. Members of the *upper* classes—hereditary or moneyed—are free in this sense, and it is by virtue of this freedom that such classes are *privileged*. The privilege is a consequence of the security that property establishes and of the power, which flows from the possession of property, over the deference and the services of others not equally blessed.

Persons qualified by this servility need not in every case be bondsmen. The servility may be intrinsic, potent within democratic society, and even re-enforced by democratic institutions. The Greeks and Romans, whose economy was grounded on slavery, had a strong feeling that many human beings are slaves by nature. As Aristotle put it, such a slave is "a tool with life in it," even as "a tool is a lifeless slave." The Russian physiologist Pavlov, who discerned and elaborated the "conditioned reflex" which has become the nuclear conception of so much contemporary psychologizing, claims to have discovered "a reflex of slavery," at least in dogs, and it may be that he has in mind the same thing that the ancients meant when they spoke of natural slaves among humans. Beings so qualified, like dairy cattle and other animals man has remade to serve his own ends, would be free only in the setting compatible with the fulfillment of their slavish propensities. Elsewhere their passions would be blocked, their natures frustrated. If there are many such intrinsically servile natures among mankind, the industrial establishment by its organization provides them with Utopian opportunities for freedom.

Perhaps it is the race's bad luck, but the historic record does not indicate that the number of slaves by nature, if they exist at all, is great among the children of man. In the large and in the small the record is far more readily one of constant straining at the leash, of evasion and struggle and rebellion and innovative charge, than of submission and acquiescence. Submission there is, but it exists as habit acquired, not as instinct inborn. It is a habit bred by the fear of insecurity, of biological dearth, and physical imbalance. Where the comparative certainty of food and clothing and shelter are lacking, freedom is also lacking. For inasmuch as men are constrained by their natures to pursue these goods, alternatives are closed to them; they seek what they must, not what they may. The modern stress upon security is a consequence of the wider-spread recognition of the fact that a free society is improbable where the individual is not assured of the minimum of food, clothing, shelter, protection against disease and against old age which are requisite for physical and mental health. When the energies of men are used entirely in fighting off starvation, they cannot be said to be free at all. They are bound to indispensables as wild animals are, and their lives are exhausted in the bare struggle to survive. If civilization is anything more than animal, it is more by the addition of wants over and above such indispensables, by the multiplication of secondary and tertiary and remoter goods between which individuals may choose. If culture has grown and spread, it has done so upon an increasingly firmer foundation of security regarding supplies for the basic wants. In nothing human is freedom as manifest as in culture, and culture is a function of prosperity. It is not necessity which has been the mother of invention, but freedom. This freedom begins where economic necessity ends. For proof, consider the leaders of revolutionary movements, the innovators in the works and ways of men, the champions of free speech and free thought. You will find them to have been, as a rule, members of the upper, the privileged classes, not of the unprivileged.

199

IV

Does it seem a paradox that, in civilization, security is a prerequisite to freedom? Then the paradox extends through all the levels of the psychophysical organization of the human personality itself. The mechanisms which make for freedom and security have been studied in animals and in infants. Pavlov drew his notions about the "reflex of slavery" from his study of the functions of the higher centers in the nervous system of the dog. The contrary "reflex of freedom" upon which he also descants is drawn from the same source. John Watson and his followers analyzed the behavior of infants and claim to have come upon certain apparently primary emotions which can be fruitfully treated as the elemental components of all elaborated and complex reactions of human beings to one another.

In the light of the Pavlovian-Watsonian observations, security might be described as the consequence of any condition whatsoever in which the psychophysical organism feels itself being supported. With the earliest instance, the support is physical. Let it be withdrawn from any infant, so that the latter will feel itself to be falling, and it will at once and automatically manifest fear. In the course of a lifetime, this reaction to the withdrawal of physical support becomes generalized. It is modified into the variety of specific responses to the withdrawal of anything which may be called a support—emotional, intellectual, material. It is nuclear in all aversion to change, whether of the conditions and practices of religion, business, politics, sport, art, and even science. It is the why of men's first reactions to innovations as fearful and avertive; why they are thrown into panic when such changes and innovations are felt to be actually shifting the ground under their mental or moral feet. Both their understanding and their firm basis of right and wrong then fail them. Without spiritual support, men, even with their material feet on the ground, cannot go about their business in peace. They manifest the same behavior as the Watsonian infant from which support is being withdrawn.

Contrasted with the withdrawal of support is the hampering of movement. Both Pavlov's dogs and Watson's babies seems to have responded to such handling in a like manner. Watson describes the response in terms of rage. In the same way as the reaction to the withdrawal of physical support becomes nuclear for reactions to the withdrawal of any support whatsoever, the rage stimulated by hampering physical movement becomes the nuclear response to the hampering of any movement whatsoever, psychological or material. With the development of the personality this response becomes, like its contrary and correlate, overlaid and inhibited, but the elemental rage which is its primal component can always be discerned. Observe it in yourself when you feel yourself being held back for any cause—the constriction of a subway crowd, the slowness of a vehicle making you late for an appointment, the stupidity of an interlocutor, the insolence of office, or the law's delays. In each and every case you feel rising in you that asphyxiate irritation, that tendency to punch and push and scream and kick and smash things which are among the stigmata of rage. In one way or another, you must throw off the binding, stifling pressure. Evidently, the organism requires from the outset a certain minimum of open space to move in freely. Experience with the world may lead us to repress this desire for open space, for freedom literal and figurative, but repression does not destroy what it represses. The repressed responses merely find another channel of discharge and manifest themselves in irritability, anger, social discontent, perversities of conduct, neurotic conservatism,

201

or radicalism of thought, and so on, endlessly. All such reaction formations are compensatory movements tending to
drain off the energy of the repressed natural hunger. Sometimes it happens that the power that withdraws support at
the same time hampers movement. Then, in the individual
heart, murder is in the making; in society, revolution.

V

The psychophysical cravings for support and room operate, it is by no means unlikely, as the prime movers of those
social philosophies which are usually described as revolutionary. If, since the beginnings of the industrial economy,
they tend to lay greater stress on equality than on freedom,
it is because industry has greatly expanded the space of
men's lives but unstabilized their support, heightening the
feeling of insecurity far beyond the feeling of unfreedom.

In the light of infant behavior, indeed, the need for security is a prior need. The baby must be supported before
it can suck and gurgle and thrust and kick. Adult individuals and social groups similarly depend upon a certain
security as prerequisite to the elaboration of conduct and
variation of behavior which compose the necessities of
civilization. This is what the *equality* of the revolution-
aries—whether Rousseauist, Marxist, or any other *ist*—
postulates. This equality is not internal sameness, but external parity. Internal sameness is impossible. First and last
each human being is an individual living his life from his
own exclusive center of being, which can never coincide
with any other. But external parity is an attainable ideal.
Possessions can be measured in terms of one another, even
though possessors are incommensurable and are compared
and ranked only by means of possessions. Where the dy-

namic difference is due to possessions only, equalization is possible. Thus the slogan of battle and defiance, "All men are created equal," is, even on Rousseau's tongue, a cry in the economic, not the metaphysical, night. It intends alone equality of possessions, that is, security.

This, I suspect, is why equality figures so recurrently as a premise to freedom. Indeed, some social philosophies such as Communism would, in theory at least, sacrifice freedom to equality. "To all according to their needs and from all according to their powers" is a commandment resting upon an unconscious faith that needs and powers are independent variables, that men are substantially alike in their needs, however different they may be in their abilities. And who shall say that with respect to the general foundations of a vital economy—the needs for food and clothing and shelter and protection against disease—this faith is altogether false?

It is when we pass from the general to the living particular that the fallacy due to dividing needs and powers becomes apparent. Even a Communist would not provide for a boy with a musical talent in the same way as for a boy with an aptitude for machinery. Biologically, every power is a need. True, producing violins and pianos and sheet music and the like in order to release the power of the nascent musician is not in principle so different from producing corn and beef and eggs in order to assuage the pangs of hunger. But who shall say that a musician is hungry in the same way as a farmer, or that his powers can be sustained and exercised on the same nourishment? Do not variant powers require different diets as well as different tools, and often receive them? If *man ist was man isst* be a true saying, *man isst was man ist* can hardly be altogether false.

Perhaps such considerations were in the minds of those

203

who found it needful to convert the simple notion of *Equality* into the more complex one of *Equality of Opportunity*. Sentimentally this maxim implied that the prizes of life were open to all who chose to try for them, that no one was cut off from trying. Any American might be President, assuming that the Presidency is a prize. But practically and logically, this implication does not work out. To work out it depends upon men's having the same ends. Such a sameness is what we establish in, for example, a foot race, where all the runners are running in order to be first to cross the line. Their opportunities are equal because it is arranged that they start from the same line at the same time over an open and uniform track upon which each man runs as fast as he can and the fastest passes the rest. Unfortunately, runners differ with respect to more things than speed, and even a uniform track may prove an unequal one. In actual life men do not pursue the same ends or chase the same rainbow. The runner in a foot race supplies no analogy for the farmers, factory hands, teachers, doctors, musicians, carpenters, psychologists, and plumbers whose incommensurable skills and functions define their diverse social and personal goals.

For these diversities to enjoy equality of opportunity calls for such an arrangement of associative relationships as will enable each variation to realize itself, to come to its fulfillment as such. Obviously, it is not a uniformity of environment that can equalize opportunities among differents; it is diversity of environment.

The social process sets up such diverse environments for individuals as configurations of group interests resulting from the mutual conflicts and adjustments of those interests. When the interests confront each other, so that an individual realizes them as alternatives between which he may choose, he is liberated from the constriction of an exclusive domination or ruling passion. Their conflict is his freedom.

It is true that their configurations continue to falsify the promise of the life more abundant which is potential in them. But this deficiency is not intrinsic; it but follows from the failure of society to set up in institutional form that elementary general security which is the underlying premise of opportunity. Health, with whatever health may require, as nourishment, clothing, and shelter; continuity of activity, with whatever continuity may require of insurance against disemployment and incapacitation—these are among the first conditions of general security. It is because industrial society so conspicuously lacks them that the theorists have underscored the security which is equality.

VI

This situation, by its inherent logic, prescribes the one wise policy which any factory, as an item of the industrial economy, may pursue with regard to freedom. A plant which is managed with due regard for its own stability and growth cannot fail to be managed with due vigilance toward the two basic psychophysical drives which move its human personnel—the drive for security and the drive for freedom.

As the psychology of our time has discerned and reported on these drives they are, both through their repression and their gratification, among the most potent of the strains and stresses that gave shape to our social economy. That no enterprise can long ignore them and survive is attested by the fact that most do ignore them and do not survive. The mortality among business enterprises is astounding: few live as long as a single man; most go under with the trough of the well-known business cycle, which is itself largely conditioned upon an inhibition of either the passion for support or the passion for freedom.

VII

Now an industrial plant is a complicated hierarchical structure whose intrinsic function is to transform a definite raw material into a definite consumable commodity as cheaply, as swiftly, as excellently as possible. This holds for the plant that transforms chicle to chewing gum as for that which converts crude iron into locomotives. Left to itself, each such plant would continue to produce greater and greater quantities of its end product in greater and greater perfection, at lesser and lesser cost, in shorter and shorter times. Its ideal engineering limit would be that instant creation out of nothing which is usually reserved for God. Inasmuch, however, as raw materials have a certain refractoriness and implements a certain inadequacy, and the wills and imagination of men a fairly apparent fallibility, the plant is obstructed from attaining the engineering limit, and God remains the undisputed monarch of his reservation.

Besides these inward limitations upon a plant's attaining the ideal fulfillment of its capacity, there are outer ones. First, there is the market, the body of customers whose needs perhaps brought the plant into existence and whose satisfactions sustain it as a going, and growing, concern. Second, there are the absentee owners, the bondholders and stockholders with whose money it was set up and put to work, and for whom ostensibly it must earn dividends and interest. Third, it may have creditors of another order—banks who have lent it money on the security of its present possessions rather than future income, and by whom it is therefore held under peonage. Fourth, there is the management itself, with the peculiar mentality deriving from its functions and powers, seeing itself as greater and more worthy of reward than pope or prince. Remember what fabulous salaries and bonuses—how much greater than those of presidents, governors, mayors, and other elective officials who manage whole nations, states, and cities with interests endlessly varied and great—railroad, bank, insurance, and other captains of Big Business modestly accept. Last only come the orders of operatives in the plant, the workers whose life force and skill *are* the industry, since when those are lacking the most cunning machine is no more than just so much curiously piled-up, good-for-nothing junk.

Now our industrial mores maintain in managers, owners, creditors, the first charge upon industry; managements feel and are expected to feel responsible first of all for profits, interest, dividends. These are expected to remain constant though wages are cut and to go on though wages stop. And in the main those expectations are met. The world being what it is, the task is far from easy. It cannot be performed without due attention to the market. Whence it comes that selling, with all which selling implies—winning customers from competitors, advertising, "high pressure salesmanship" —tends in the long run to take precedence over production as a responsiblity of the management. Making to sell becomes paramount over making to satisfy needs. Since the experience of the past quarter of the century has sufficiently established that—as in the typical case of the wooden nutmeg—this paramountcy is by no means an unambiguous advantage, even bankers dictating production policies have tended to reduce the paramountcy to a parity. In the present-day conduct of bona fide business, production thus often has an equal voice with advertising and sales.

Remarkable as it may seem to souls chiefly aware of business enterprise through salesmen, the quality of goods depends upon the processes of production, upon their constant modification and improvement in the light of the intrinsic ends of the industry. But modification and improvement call for continuous initiative, for experimentation, for in-

207

novations and trials costing great sums which the sales must return. Let the record of the house of Ford testify. Aiming to produce for his market at a profit, Henry Ford arrested the improvement of his goods during a score of years. He standardized the technique, the tools, the product and sought by rapid repetition to pay himself back a million-fold the initial cost of his initiative and invention. Now the times have overtaken him, and he has been compelled to innovate and experiment again. Whether he can delay improving change so long and with the same impunity is a doubtful question. The automotive industry as a whole has too great a momentum.[1]

The case of Ford is typical of every new variant which enters the industrial economy. What meaning has it for freedom in the factory? No one will want to deny that initiative, experimentation, and endeavor after new materials, new devices, and new methods that shall make goods at once cheaper and more excellent are forms of freedom in industry. But how removed is this freedom from the necessity of the repetitive processes of quantity production! The latter imposes uniformity of act and thought. And how can such a uniformity fail to shut out alternatives, to stereotype, and thus work as a hampering of movement and an antagonist of freedom? That there are hosts of workers who prefer the security of monotonous repetition over the expansiveness and risk of realistic initiative and experiment, I recognize. These men and women take their freedom through compensatory daydreaming, which Elton Mayo studied, and not a few among their number find indispensable a per-

---

[1] Since these lines were written, the newspapers reported that Ford felt compelled by competitive pressure once more to innovate and improve. The situation contained the dynamics for a disintegratingly rapid tempo, with the bankruptcy of the Ford company for its limit. The company's alternative was to keep up with the Joneses of the motor industry, and it more or less has.

iodic disinhibition by means of alcohol and other narcotics. They must have jags in order to carry on their lives. But the number of all such is not as great as sentimentalists expect. Most workers thrive better as operatives and as men when they have freedom on the job as well as security in the job. Psychological tests seem to indicate that the optimal condition for any activity whatsoever exists when variety and repetition occur in a broad ratio of one to two.

VIII

Can such a condition be established in a modern industrial plant? Well, look at its structure and organization. It is an arrangement whereby different tools tended or employed by different people with different skills and functions are applied to carry on different processes whose *terminus ad quem* is a commodity ready for use and consumption. The processes compose an ordered series, the later ones depending on all the earlier in such a way that a failure at any one phase arrests the movement of each and all. The differents are more than organically interdependent. A man need not stop living when a leg or arm or nerve stops functioning, but a plant must drop a working whenever any single step in its serial process fails to come off. The serial nature of the process, the interdependence of its phases is such that a perfectly Taylored plant should go as smoothly and uninterruptedly as an electric clock. And if it could be as independent of the intervention and interpolation of human energies, it would do so. But that high place of the cult of efficiency is still, if not in the impossible, in the remote future. Men must intervene with brain and hand, must interpolate their energies at this point and that of the channel for material energy which the automatic machine impatterns.

Now men are discontinuous individual personalities, each

with his idiosyncratic, incommensurable living rhythm, only perilously to be synchronized to the impersonal automatic machine. Nevertheless the machine imposes upon all who work at it an unwonted and unwanted interdependence; making by its very nature the activities of all conditional upon the activities of each, it conforms men into relationships so alien to their inward essence and habit of life as to be difficult to realize and more difficult to accept. The class solidarity, class consciousness, and class war which the socialist gospel promulgates remain for the most part seed cast upon barren ground.

Yet the gospel expresses associative actualities of industry which the last detached observer acknowledges. It envisages and voices however alone the pressure of automatic machinery upon human association. It does not envisage and voice the human heart. Men feel themselves first and last as individuals, not as particulars of a class. And in their relations with one another, whether as employee with employee or employee with employer, they so comport themselves. The incompatibilities between the nature of man and the works of the industrial establishment have thus far given employers an invidious advantage: the worker's nature has worked on the employer's side against the worker's interests. It has exposed him to those very insecurities which taking a job presumably saves him from. But having ceased these hundred years from farming, he is no longer saved by working alone. His job now imposes associative conditions, and hence his security requires them. Security is now a consequence of collaboration, conscious or unconscious. It is now a collective fact, guaranteeable only by conscious collective action. Only in the degree that this exists can the full possibilities of factory production be actualized, and men reassured industrially in their instinctual need of support. Upon such support, so established, freedom could grow.

At first glance, there are two directions for the growth of freedom in the environment of the factory. One is that taken by the saints and sages of religion and philosophy. Its essence is an acquiescence based on adequate and passionate knowledge, on a participation of heart and head in the total process of an industry. For the most part, the well-known division of labor has brought only a narrowing of consciousness and a constriction of intention. Workers are required to perform their special tasks without looking behind, before, or around. They are kept unaware of the nature and origin of their tools and materials, of the linkage of their operations with those preceding and following, of the role of their action in the character of the terminal result, of its dynamic connection with the action of their fellow workers. Some never see the terminal result. They are placed at their station, like common soldiers trained only to obey: "Theirs not to reason why, theirs but to do and die."

For these the way to freedom in the factory is the way of technologically reasoning why, of expanding their vision from their own narrow task to the entire operation in which the factory as a whole is the craftsman and the worker but one of its hands. Whatever else industrial democracy could mean it could not mean anything less than this participative realization of the entire process of production, its conditions, its means, and its results. When each and every worker is aware of the purposes and problems of the plant as a whole, when he realizes himself as an individual contributing his own skills and power and playing a personal part in the upkeep and growth of the whole, and as sharing in its control and fortunes, he ceases to be a hand unwillingly coerced and becomes a man freely co-operating. His state

211

of mind—which is customarily both servile and rebellious, as might be that of a horse drawing a wagon under the giddap and lash of the driver, who for his labors supports him —becomes that independent and co-operative one characteristic of a team of men playing at football or baseball or any other sport. The depressed attitude of "Thy will, not mine" is lifted up into "Our will—thine and mine. . . ." Whatever form democracy may take in industry, it works toward freedom only if and as it enables the worker to identify himself with the entire industry as a teammate, a free participant in the concerns of the whole.

The second avenue to freedom in the factory supplements the first. It is the opportunity to experiment, to take initiative, to exercise, and to gratify the creative impulse under conditions of competitive co-operation. This calls for an organization of the productive setup on the basis that, whatever be a worker's place and duties within its structure, variations, novelties and improvements are both possible and desirable in his part of the job. The chance to experiment and to choose between alternative patterns of execution would need to be as integral a part of the plant's structure as its organization for invariant repetition. Where a worker's intervention in the machine process is reduced to the minimum of tendance, the range of variation and choice is extremely narrow; but even there opportunities are not lacking. At least an order of competitive excellence is possible such as runners aim at in a race, and slight modifications of form are by no means unlikely. On jobs less restricted and standardized, anything which stimulates variation, initiative, discrimination, and selection both enhances freedom and enriches industry. It calls into play another component of our orginal nature—the manipulative passion which matures into what Veblen called the "instinct of workmanship." The repression of this instinct seems to have been less dangerous than the repression of others but has brought its unmistakable consequences. In its release and gratification we open up another, perhaps more precious if less funda- mental, road to freedom in the factory.

Free Enterprise
and the Consumer

THE WORD *future* stands for the most comprehensive and momentous of our interests. Not a thing we do, not a thing we say but gets its meaning in that which is not yet but which grows out of it. Whether we are dealing with Today or with Yesterday, their import for us and for our survival lies in Tomorrow. The entire business of life, we might say, is to anticipate Tomorrow. To discern, to foretell, to prepare for the future is the all of science, of art, of government, and of religion. And the irony is that if that which we seek is unprecedented, new, genuinely future, we cannot predict it, whereas if it repeats the past, so that we can anticipate events as we do the turns of the sun and the seasons, our foreknowledge is not prophecy of the new but assurance about the old. And this, I am afraid, is all the power over the future the gods have ever allowed us— especially the future of freedom. All we possess to guide us to Freedom's tomorrow is Freedom's yesterday. And that which we know about Freedom's yesterday is not too encouraging. Perhaps our culture has had in recent years no concern so momentous to its survival as freedom. President Roosevelt had designated a fourfold province for it when he counted the aims of life and the fruits of victory as "The Four Freedoms," and assigned to each of them a share for tomorrow consisting but of a repetition and an

214

extension of their yesterday. Whatever meaning the Four now have inheres in that yesterday, and whatever new meaning tomorrow may join to yesterday is unpredictable. If it comes at all it will come as a free gift. Before it can be employed as a yardstick of necessity or a measure of reason, it will enter experience as an awareness of grace. The knowledgeable future is and ever has been a repetition and prolongation of the past. The innovative future is beyond knowledge: it transcends inference: it may present itself to intuition, but intuition cannot seek it out. It is that which those who become aware of it really mean when they say *revelation.* It is news in the sense in which the events of evolution are news, in the sense in which man would have been news to the apelike ancestors from which he descends. Imagine these ancestors discussing the future. How could they have thought of it save as an apelike future? The transformations toward humanity perforce were dark events that they resisted and shut out. Struggling for their own survival, they struggled for their continuation as apes, not for their extinction into men.

And does not the same thing hold in our own struggle to live and to grow as the kinds of human beings we feel we are? The future we seek is not one that will transform or abolish us, but one that will perfect and fulfill us; a future in which we become more abundantly and beautifully the beings we are, not one which replaces us with another species. And to us as we are, freedom is the innermost value; the future we desire and would attain is the state in which freedom flourishes in every shape that may enchannel it: in the shape of thought and expression, in the shape of faith and worship, in the shape of political and social and economic self-rule, in the shape of the wisdom that is courage concerning dangers. To us as we are, future existence is delineated by present plan. On the

record, we Americans possess a ground plan of such existence upon which most others had come to base themselves,
from which many others are derivations, of which many
others are contradictions. This ground plan is a statement
about human nature and human relations, about the bearing of human institutions upon this nature and these relations, and about the ways in which human nature shapes
and is shaped by human institutions. The plan was laid
down in 1776. It is to my feeling the foremost document in
the National Bible of Freedom, but it has been felt as the
charter of liberty everywhere in the world. We know it as
the Declaration of Independence. Every American and
certainly every co-operator, whether American or not, ought
to know it by heart.

Consider its simple affirmations. Not many of us think
of the impact of these propositions, which to the signers of
the Declaration were "self-evident truths," in the shaping
of the American way of life and the creation of the American spirit. Whether we know it or not they affect the conditions of our waking and our sleeping, of our eating and
drinking, of our loving and fighting, of our working and
playing. It will reward us to inquire what to be free means
in the minds of men who stake their lives and fortunes and
sacred honor on the statement that freedom is an unalienable right which therefore none can possibly take from any.
It will reward us to inquire what sense it makes to treat
freedom as thus unalienable.

Think what we do to other people's freedom! Can it be
truly said that the freedom of a person in jail has not been
alienated or that it is not an alienation of liberty to coerce
men and women through their fears and hungers, so that
they do what they do not wish and do not do what they
wish; so that they say they believe what they do not believe and do not say what they do believe? Could the sign-

ers of the Declaration have ignored experiences such as these, which are common to the generations? Of course they could not. Nor did they. The Declaration was itself a repudiation of such attempted and more or less successful alienation of liberty practiced by the goverment of England upon the peoples of the British Colonies in America. That which the signers meant by an unalienable right was a right following from our natures as men: they meant that so long as a man lived and struggled to go on living, he would struggle to be free, nor could he give over this struggle to the day he dies. They meant that by nature men would rather be free than safe. Although we hear a great deal about security—social security, economic security, military security—and the halls of Congress have been echoing the screamers of the journals in their iterations about security, yet nobody who was really secure would stay that way for a day.

I know of Utopian societies in different parts of the world that are perfections of security. Their members are well fed; their health is cared for. They are effectively clothed against the weather; they are provided with sports, entertainment, culture, and the consolations of religion. From the point of view of their guardians they are exposed to no risks and sheltered from all troubles. These Utopias are called jails. The signal fact regarding the aspirations of all their inhabitants is that they want to get out of Utopia as soon as possible. They would rather be free than safe. They would rather live among the risks that go with being in command over their own persons, their own powers, and, as far as may be, their own destiny. They would rather incur the dangers of choosing for themselves between ideas, political parties, religious denominations, diets, dwelling places, occupations, life companions, friends. They would rather draw upon their own initiative than another's rules.

They would rather get new ideas, invent new devices, than rely upon the rules or prescription of others. In all the enterprises of life they would choose freedom, and if they overstress security, they overstress it because they would use it as a facilitation of freedom.

I

The whole meaning of the ideal called free enterprise inheres in these natural preferences of natural men. Reformers, intellectuals, men and women indignant over the misery in which so many simple people live, have denounced free enterprise or sneered at it. But they have been reacting to a phrase contaminated by the hypocrisies of its users, not to a fact recorded and an ideal understood. That which in truth has moved them to indignation was not free enterprise among the many but its monopolization by the few, its blocking and damming up in the lives of the many, its transposition into monopolistic privilege in the operations of the few. Under the terms of the Declaration of Independence, no man can be completely a man who is cut off from being responsible to himself for himself and for his powers and from exercising them at his own risk, in his labors to live, to be free, and to find happiness. Under the terms of the Declaration of Independence only that society can be a free society which guarantees this equally to unequals. A free society is a society in whose works and ways liberty lives as an unalienable right so guaranteed and protected by the law that the expression of liberty and the security of the different in each other's presence are one and the same.

We might say, indeed, that the whole purpose of the Declaration was to affirm and to vindicate men's right to be different. The world to which is was addressed held anything but that. It was a world in which human beings were penalized for being different in thousands of ways. Dark-skinned men and women were penalized for the color of their skin. Women were penalized for not being men. Congregationalists, Catholics, Presbyterians, Anglicans, Baptists penalized each other for their denominational unlikenesses. The entire Christian world penalized Jews for not being Christian. Believers penalized unbelievers for believing otherwise than they. Gentlemen of leisure, who could live without working, penalized peasants and laborers, who had to work without living, merely because they existed under this necessity. Work itself, indeed, was regarded as a penalty paid for original sin, and to be a workman meant to live under the penalty, without dignity, without power, without freedom.

Hence, when the Declaration affirmed that "all men are equal," it was not affirming that all men are the same. Quite the contrary, it was affirming that men differ from each other in countless ways, and that as separate and undefeasible individualities, each unique, each different from the others, they are equal to each other in dignity, worth, and meaning. It was affirming the right to be different and the equal claim of the different on life, liberty, and the pursuit of happiness. It was implying, if not saying, that a free society is a voluntary union of the different; that men need each other not as they feel and think and act alike but as they differ, so that each can bring to the union with his neighbors something that they do not already have, a different power, a different knowledge, a different skill, a different achievement, whose free exchange generates and sustains a community of free men.

219

II

Hypothetically, every consumer enterprise is a community so constituted; every co-operative society, with its stores and fields and factories, is a community so constituted. And each has its characteristic organization of powers which may be called government. Government is a way of working together devised by the people who are different from each other in order to serve their different ends by common rules, common action, and common tools. "To secure these rights governments are instituted among men and they derive their just powers from the consent of the governed"—this proposition proclaims the very essence of democratic government, whether it be that of a village, a city, a province, a sovereign and independent state, a church, a school, a business enterprise, a scientific or artistic undertaking, or the United Nations.

But even as much that receives the name free enterprise is the opposite of free enterprise, so much that goes by the name of democracy is a repudiation and dishonor to that name. There obtain among us, also in our free American society, great economic and financial undertakings, religious establishments, and political orders which are as totalitarian as carteis and monopolies, as hierarchical as armies. Their rule is arbitrary and authoritative. They deal with men and women as if they were merely animate tools, merely beasts of burden. Whatever be the principles they profess, their practices are tyrannical. Their action postulates that the people are made by some higher power for government, not that government is made by the people for the people. Like Franco in Spain, they do not attribute their powers to the weakness or the consent of the governed, but to some superior merit in themselves. They feel themselves to be rulers by divine right, or by the power of tooth and claw which is the classical manifestation of divine right, and they enjoy their privileged liberties under divine sanctions.

Of all this the Declaration was and remains a repudiation. To all this the Declaration throws down the gage of war, war on all levels of our social existence: on the level of faith, on the level of thought and inquiry, on the level of culture and education, on the level of economic enterprise, on the level of military conflict; war at all times in all places —witness our struggle for independence, our Civil War, and our two international wars to make the world safer for democracy.

Let us pause a moment on the issues which culminated in our Civil War. They had already been defined by the author of the Declaration of Independence, who foresaw the bitter and bloody consequence of denying to men and women whose skin was black their equal right to life, liberty, and the pursuit of happiness. This denial had, in point of fact, not been limited to our darker Americans alone. White men as well as black, for one reason or another, were transposed, without their participating in the reason, from free human beings into chattel properties. Although the white men were called indentured servants and the black men were called slaves, in daily life their status in relation to their masters was the same. Between 1776 and 1789, while the nation was laboring toward its constitutional form, a great debate ran its course among the American people. They argued whether the institution of slavery and of indentured servanthood could be in any way consistent with the propositions of the Declaration of the existence of a free society. Thomas Jefferson, indeed, made the attempt to have slavery and servitude shut out from the nation's free land but failed. The members of the Constitutional Convention, as James Madison records, debated the

issue again as they moved toward the collection of com-
promises which make up the first version of the Constitution of the United States. But the power of property in men
was too strong. Behind it, supporting it, worked our age-old
way of life, which held that people who were different from
oneself are by nature inferior to oneself. The traditions of
this way were common alike to the classical and to the
Christian economy. Within them, manual labor was intrinsically servile and incapable of liberty; manual laborers
were, as Aristotle called them, "tools with life in them,"
best off as slaves and nothing else. These traditions enabled
Americans with a vested interest in servitude to secure the
constitutional perpetuation of that interest, in an enactment which "we the People of the United States" ordained
and established in order to "secure the Blessings of Liberty
to ourselves and our Posterity." Those who read the Constitution and do not merely talk about it or quote it like the
Bible will recall the words in the second section of the
Fourth Article. I set them down here for all to read:

No person held in service or labor in one state under the laws
thereof, escaping into another, shall in consequence of any law
or regulation therein be discharged from any such service or
labor, but shall be delivered up on the claim of the party to
whom the service or labor may be due.

This law applies to all persons, without distinction of race,
faith, or sex. You may call this impartially democratic if
you please. It remained in force until 1865 when the Thir-
teenth Amendment to the Constitution was adopted. That,
together with the Fourteenth and Fifteenth, purposed to
nullify the perpetuation of property in human labor. The
three amendments were intended to release all men who
work into possession of themselves as workers. The intention is still far short of realization.

222

Concurrent with this release came the upsurge of the free association of workers as workers which we call the Labor Movement. There followed the slow, uncertain march of the trade-unions to power and influence. Trade-unions had at one time been condemned as unconstitutional. The equal liberty of employees with employers to unite in order the better to defend their stake in their occupations and in the hours and condition of their labor had been continually suffering challenge, denial, and combat. Its vindication was and remains an ongoing battle. Various weapons were directed against it. One was the black list; another was the injunction. Another was the goon squad. Another was the state militia. Still another was federal troops, as many citizens of Chicago still living can recall. And there were many others. Nevertheless, slowly, if not surely, the democratic idea triumphed. A new attitude appeared among men of property and power, a new habit embodying their grudging but sure acquiescence in the equal right of workingmen to associate together as an occupational group for the purpose of assuring to themselves the just rewards of their knowledge and skill and powers in production. We call this new situation the right of collective bargaining. The yellow dog contract and the blacklegs which were used to oppose it, have practically disappeared from public discussion. We regard collective bargaining as a victory in the conquest of freedom by the common man.

And it is a victory; it is a step forward in the winning of democracy. But pause a moment before the idea. Look into its meaning. As men bargain over the price of bed or board, of shirt or shoe, so men bargain (now collectively) over the price of the strength, the skill, and the knowledge of human beings. They deal in labor as a commodity similar in nature to a ham sandwich, an ice cream cone, a powder puff, or a brassiere. They bargain for it as if it could be detached from the person of the laborer in the same way that an article of wear or diet may be taken from the shelf on which it is kept. They speak of the labor market. But they do not speak of the ineluctable fact that a man's strength and skill and knowledge are nothing and less than nothing without the man whose strength and skill and knowledge they are. Who buys these buys the man also. Who sells these sells another man or sells himself. Collective bargaining is a gain for democracy, but far from a realization of that equal and unalienable liberty of different men which the Declaration of Independence affirms. It does not envisage, far less achieve, that fundamental self-possession and freedom of choice which the Declaration holds to be inward to human nature. And this is why the struggle to establish its principles as practices did not and cannot stop with collective bargaining. This is why in due course, the struggle for freedom won a new victory and wrote a new law—a law greeted as an achievement of "the New Freedom" whose inspiration Woodrow Wilson brought to the guidance of national policy. This law is to be found in the Clayton Act. The Clayton Act, you remember, was a law further safeguarding the nation against the powers and stratagems of trusts and monopolies. It was framed to supply the deficiencies of the Sherman Act, that first law directed by Congress to the protection of the people and the people's interest from the depradations of Big Business. Its purpose was to regulate and control monopolies in transportation, manufacture, and markets. Its subject matter is things, property real and personal. But living labor was also being treated as a commodity of the market, sold and bought like a dead thing. And in order to protect the free association of laborers from the consequences of this condition, in order to guard the trade union from being treated as a trust or monopoly trading in human strength, knowledge, and skill, the Clayton Act made it the law of the land that "the labor of a human being is not a commodity or an article of commerce."

True, this affirmation was sabotaged from the day it was adopted, nor has the war against it been relaxed. Nevertheless, it has laid down a gradient of liberty. The import it carries is momentous. It acknowledges that a man's labor flows from his being, that it cannot be put off or on like a shirt or sold across a counter like a can of beans. It accepts the fact that there is no way to detach the work of a man from the person of a man and attach it to the machine. It recognizes that the man goes as and where his labor goes, and that it can never be otherwise. That "the labor of a human being is not a commodity or an article of commerce" starts with the recognition, nevertheless, that we do keep treating labor as if it were a commodity and article of commerce, as if it were independent and detachable as beans or jeans. And this implies that, even with collective bargaining, the victory of human freedom over human bondage is precarious; that a man's possession of himself is always in danger, never secure, and more so than ever in our industrial economy.

III

The reason why inheres in the character of the economy. Almost everybody knows some little shoemaker, usually an Italian, doing business in a smelly, small shop where he has his bench, his hammer and his awl, his knife and his wax, his thread and his needle. He is here today, gone tomorrow. He can pack all the tools of his trade in his handbag or on his back and move about as he wishes. His tools are extensions of his person. He can take them up, use

225

them as he chooses, then lay them down. But let him for some reason cease to be a cobbler and become a hand in a shoe factory and then his relation to his tools changes. His tools are no longer a function of his person. On the contrary, his person becomes an extension of a tool which is not his. To all intents and purposes he becomes a human gadget attached at a certain point to a stationary machine. He must act as the machine requires. He is not free to take it up or put it down. He cannot make it go according to his own organic rhythm. He is compelled to conform his own rhythm to that of the machine and God help him should his attention flag from conformation. As a cobbler, he could make a whole pair of shoes, shaping part to part and shoe to foot, in a complete continuing organic act. As a shoe operative he is but one among thirty or forty or a hundred other human beings each performing a separate and distinct operation which together work out into a complete shoe. As an operative not he, the man, is the shoemaker, making a whole pair of shoes. It is the factory which is the shoemaker. The man is but $\frac{1}{30}$ or $\frac{1}{40}$ or $\frac{1}{100}$ of the shoemaker. By taking a place in the industrial structure he has cut down his stature as a whole man. His humanity has been submerged in his economic function. He has become one type of the abstraction, economic man—a mere laborer, a producer without any personal relation to that which he produces, a container of human energy, to be burnt like gas in an engine, in order to make the wheels go round.

What now, I ask, becomes of the rest of his being? What becomes of the son and brother, the lover, the husband, the father, the sportsman, the citizen, the music lover, the reader, the theatregoer, the churchman? What becomes of all the many, many, other interests which flow together to make up the life of the simplest man? Also the farmer who by and large, even the poorest, has been able to lead a completer, freer, more human existence than the industrial worker, undergoes an analogous transformation, as agriculture becomes industrialized. Also the farmer tends to be diminished from a man using a machine into a gadget used by a machine, a man conformed to its rhythms, merely earning his living instead of living his life, so that his mentality is cut down to a mere earner's mentality.

Literature is full of testimonies to the pity of this situation, with its tragic paradoxes and ironic contradictions. Adam Smith, Thomas Jefferson, Carlyle, Ruskin, Marx, Robert Owen, Ira Stewart, Charles Fourier, Henry Thoreau, Edward Bellamy, and hundreds upon hundreds of essayists and novelists as well have borne testimony to this contraction and diminution of the complex humanity of western man.

Perennially, for example, we hear lamentations about unemployment, and never perhaps such minatory ones as those of this day. We hear them from employers and employees and their trade-union leaders alike. We hear about a "right to work" and "full employment." But when we ask, "What, in the life of any worker or in the policy of any trade-union, do these experiences mean?" then we learn that they seek ever higher and higher wages and ever shorter and shorter hours. Policy, we find, calls on the one hand for full employment and on the other for reducing employment to a minimum. Trade unionists are denounced hence for greed and hypocrisy. But neither employees nor college professors, nor yet government officials ever stop to study what are the forces which underly a predicament so patent that those who are stuck in it have no awareness of the paradox they embody. This paradox flows from the dehumanization of men, from identifying the organization of things with the relations of human beings to themselves and to one another.

The fact is that men, free men, are not by nature working-men. They are not by nature producers. They are by nature consumers and are distorted into producers by necessity. That we are consumers, and consumers first, last, and all the time, is obvious enough during the infancy of even the poorest and the late years of everybody who lives to be old. But at a certain stage in the biography of most of us, our needs as consumers drive us into becoming producers. If we are able to go on living we fall under the necessity of working. But we don't go to work for the fun of it; we go to work for a living. The hog must root or die. But he does not die from not rooting, he dies from not eating. Those among us whom Providence has blessed with an income so that they can live without working do not die from not working. But I would be willing to bet that nobody will take a bet, even at a thousand to one, that they will not die from not eating. It isn't those who don't work who perish; it is those who don't eat who perish. If men could eat without working, who would work? Work is a necessary evil. It is a burden imposed on our lives by the nature of the world we live in, and every religion, every philosophy has its own interpretation of the origin of this evil.

Those who are familiar with the Christian interpretation will recall the Eden story. The Garden of Eden may be said to symbolize the primal economy of human life. It was a consumer economy, an economy of abundance. Adam and Eve did not begin their careers as man and woman in the role of producers. They began their careers in the role of consumers. Divine providence had provided them with everything save knowledge of good and evil. A tree bearing the fruit of this grew in Eden, but our first parents were commanded not to eat thereof. Satan persuaded them to disobey the commandment. They did eat, and the Lord cursed them and expelled them from Eden. He also cursed

228

the earth unto which he drove them forth. He established the economy of scarcity under which man has travailed ever since—an earth which would of itself bring forth only thorns and thistles, a human race which could earn its bread only by labor, only in the sweat of its face. This is why labor is a necessary evil. It is the divine curse. It is the penalty for disobedience. It is tied in to a natural scarcity. Both are symbolic of Adam's sin and evidence of the fall of man. And the children of Adam have always looked upon labor as a curse. Nobody who goes to work looks forward, when he begins his career as a workingman, to remaining a workingman all his life. He dreams a dream—a writer of history speaks of "the American dream"—that the time may come soon, when he shall have earned and saved and won enough to enable him to stop working and start living. That dream animates his personal ambitions and social revolutions; it invests imagined Utopias with glamour and reform movements with force. It gives their character to most conceptions of heaven, which is by definition one unending Sabbath of delighted consummation.

The multitudes of us dreamers, nevertheless, born consumers as we are, do after a short time become producers as well. And to the day we die we are under the necessity to work without living, while a minority among us are privileged by birth, station, and property to live without working.

To live, to be free, to pursue happiness—these unalienable rights of the American vision of man—do they imply man the producer or man the consumer? Does the new "right to work" envisage man living or man earning a livelihood, man doing freely what he wishes or doing what he would not do if he didn't have to? Is "the pursuit of happiness" a synonym for the hours spent on the job earning a wage? Let us envisage a moment of an American working

day, say your own. You are in bed asleep. The factory whistle blows, your alarm clock goes off, you wake reluctantly.
You get out of bed as slowly as you dare. You yawn. You
stretch. If you shave, you do so in a very futuristic way. You
dress in your work clothes. You bolt a breakfast, and
you hurry off, perhaps in the dark, to your place in the factory, or in the cow barn to serve the needs of those purely
consumer cows. If your place is in a factory, then every day
and all day long, you probably repeat just one movement
over and over and over again, until the whistle advises you
that it is time for lunch. The power turns off. You leave your
station on the assembly line. Perhaps you wash your hands;
perhaps you feel unwilling to take the time. If there is a
lunchroom maintained by the shop, perhaps you go there;
perhaps you've brought your own and do not buy but find a
corner where you may eat. Or perhaps you are one of those
myriads who these days stand four deep before drugstore
lunch counters, who feed and move on, feed and move on,
in sequences resembling those of their operations on the
production line. They swallow lunch as they bolted breakfast. Perhaps they are able to pause a moment for a ciga-
rette. But before an hour is over, all are back in their places
on the line.

What, in sober fact, did eating this lunch amount to? It
certainly did not amount to consuming a human meal. It
amounted only to restoking a physiological engine. The
morning's work had burned up the caloric intake called
breakfast, and perhaps more. The noon meal replaced that
burnt-up fuel, to be burnt up in its turn by the afternoon's
labor. At last, a whistle blows; it is sundown or later. The
day's work stops; production ceases. The change that follows is so habitual, so customary, that the paradoxical nature of it passes unnoticed. But it consists in fact of a series
of self-transformations that reach their height in a variety of

230

activities having in common with the day's occupation only the fact that they are performed by the same individual. When the whistle blows and the machines stop, you give over doing whatever you are doing. You put away your tools. You take off your work clothes. You wash away the grime and sweat of the day from your body—sometimes also the blood and tears. You clothe yourself in other clothes. At last you sit down to your evening meal. This is the third time you eat, but it is the first time you eat like a human being instead of merely stoking up a physiological engine. That which you eat may be no different in kind and caloric value from what you ate for breakfast and lunch, although usually it is much more varied. But the way in which you eat it is immensely different. For you are now released from the yoke you wore while earning your living. You are, for the moment, free to be living your life. You have shifted from producing to consuming, from earning to spending. You are under no compulsion to bolt your food. You are under no pressure to disregard the dishes and the service. You can take your time to sit at a table covered with a clean cloth, laid with shining silver and plates and cups and glasses that are shaped and decorated to please the eye as well as to hold the food and drink. Flowers, perhaps, enrich the table pattern. The family radio gives news or music as you eat. You converse with wife and children or with friends. When the meal is over, perhaps you read the newspapers, or even a book; perhaps you go to a church service or a political rally or a lodge meeting, or perhaps you prefer a movie or a pool parlor or a bowling alley, or a skating rink or even a dance hall. Perhaps you roll up the carpets and dance to a radio or phonograph at home. Perhaps you sit down to a game of poker or gin rummy.

You can win a lot of money at poker or gin. But unless you are a professional gambler you would hardly call play-

231

ing such games a method of earning a living or production. Nor would you describe any of the things you do at night, when the day's work is over, in that way. You would feel them as being, by contrast, free, as being what you do when you are having fun. The good of them is, first and last, in what they are as they go on, not in what they produce when they have stopped. They are actions of leisure, not of labor. They are that which you live for and come alive in. They make up your night life, and your day life consists in securing the means to your night life. By day you are but a producer. At night you are the consumer you were born to be.

IV

In our industrial civilization night life is now become synonymous with all the goods and services we appreciate as culture—the theater, the concert, the lecture, the public meeting, the cocktail or dinner party. Almost every event we value, except the job, is an event of the night. We work by day in order that we may live by night. We are bond by day in order that we may be free by night. And not a man, not a woman, exists who is healthy in body and mind who would not prefer to be free by day as well as by night. One might say, indeed, that the inwardness of the human struggle for freedom is to restore to our day life the consummatory character now so largely restricted to night life. Somehow, the consumer each was born as has been aborted into the producer he has had to become lest he perish. Somehow, the spirit of man inveterately resists this abortion, and labors and fights to shape a society in which human nature may recover and perfect its consummatory essence.

How may this be done? Various devices are proposed, Utopian and reformist. In many cases—such as those of present-day Russia and of Nazi Germany—the cure has served to make the disease only more horrible and corrupt. It has converted labor from a necessary evil consequent in the nature of things into a planned enslavement consequent on the will-to-power and greed of ruthless men. It has converted an economic structure that is to be found in several forms and many sizes in relatively free societies into one huge totalitarian organization with enterprise co-ordinated to enterprise as regiment is co-ordinated to regiment in an army. I refer, of course, to the trust or corporation whose role in the American way has been to bring on a new alienation of the unalienable liberty of men and women, not only economic but intellectual and political as well.

For example, it is chiefly the spokesmen for our corporations who proclaim the virtues of free enterprise and who announce the efforts of government to protect those virtues as unconstitutional blockings of the very life stream of the American way. But what have they in mind when they say *free enterprise?* Do they have in mind the equal right of little people to engage in little business at their own risk? If they have, how can they reconcile this conception of free enterprise with the proved and established charge that Big Business consistently employs all the devices of ruthless competition—i.e., of fraud and force—to drive the competitor out of business and to take the entire field for itself alone? Be the enterprise General Foods, General Electric, or General Motors, this willy-nilly is the disposition of the interest it embodies. Between only December, 1941, and December, 1943, 1,078,000 individual, private, free enterprises failed. There are more than 500,000 fewer private undertakers—and I do not mean morticians. What becomes of these *failures?* What becomes of these Americans who paid the price of private initiative and free enterprise not because they were ignorant or incompetent or dishonest, but because the competition which defeated them owns a financial power so great that it is like an earthquake or a tidal wave, which breaks up or sweeps away what it encounters not by virtue of greater wisdom or competitive excellence but by the sheer weight of material power. If the victims of this power survive it, they become its servants. Their liberty passes from them to the employing corporation. The more Americans come to depend for their livelihood on these establishments the more control over the wills of the American people the corporations attain. Three hundred and fifty thousand of our countrymen are thus open to the control of the United States Steel Corporation, five hundred thousand to that of General Motors. In 1940 one hundred corporations received 86 per cent of the government's contracts; in 1943 this fell to only 70 per cent; in 1944 thirty-one corporations operated more than half of all the government's plants. Out of the Federal Department of Justice have come repeated warnings from men like Thurman Arnold, Walton Hamilton, Wendel Rogge, that these corporations conduct themselves in industry as sovereign states do in politics. Concerned only over the monopolies of making, selling, and buying products and taking profits and over the bearing of the corporate structure on the power of property thus resulting, the officials have laid much less stress on the relation of man to man within that corporate structure. But to those concerned over the future of freedom, it is this relation that wants special emphasis.

I stress therefore that a corporation tends to take the shape and build of a small-scale corporative state. A country whose economy corporations dominate, whose government either has not the will or cannot muster the power to police and regulate them so as to safeguard the free enterprise and private initiative of the people, is destined to pass over from this piecemeal fascism to a full dress fascist state, like Russia today. This is why trade-unions must be strong enough to meet the mightiest of corporations head on. And this is why the power of government in industrialized democracies should always be different from and greater than that of any other structure or institution in the national life. The alternative is finis to the liberties of the people.

For as corporations are at present organized and conducted, each is a hierarchy of the fascist type. Its pattern is military. Men and women who enter its service are set in formations where decisions are authoritarian. They are placed at stations where they must do things whose relations to the doings of others they know not. They are permitted to be *in* the plant or industry but not *of* it. Its affairs are not supposed to be their affairs, nor their destiny its destiny. They are constrained to serve in occupational blinkers, without any awareness of the interdependence of their tasks, or the interrelations of the plant and industry with the other aspects of the national economy. This knowledge is the monopoly of the directorate and management; as for the men—theirs not to reason why; theirs but to work and die.

It is this enforced unawareness, this shutting-out from participation in knowing and planning which, under the inescapable interdependence that follows from the division of labor, renders a workingman more than ever bond and not free, a producer merely and not a consumer. For knowledge and participation are consummatory. Converting coercion into consent, they set free. The free man is the man who knows what he is doing and why. He is aware of the structure and dynamics of the industry in which his vocation is a function. He knows how it meshes into the national economy. He understands the conditions of its survival and prosperity. He participates in the making of its

235

policies. By his vote he counts in it equally with all others as one, and never as more than one, however large may be his proprietary interest; and never less than one, however small or absent his share as owner.

This is of course the first rule and final practice in the government of democratic states. Every citizen, regardless of race, color, sex, faith, wealth, or occupation, is entitled to a vote in the choice of his country's officers and lawmakers. In the determination of its policies and program, his opinions, his desires, and his needs receive preponderant consideration. It is in this relation to his government that his citizenship consists. Yet, accepted beyond challenge as good enough to function as a citizen of his nation, he is shut out and cut off from citizenship in the industry wherein he earns his living. There, he remains still, as Aristotle defined the slave, "a tool with life in it," a means of production, an energy device made of living matter attached to a machine made of dead matter, and harnessed to the pattern of its motions and rhythm. His dignity and worth as a human being are subdued to his uses as a physiological mechanism; his powers and skills are checkreined to production and ridden by a will not his own to ends he does not know and is kept from sharing. Whereas, were the same tasks freely chosen, illumined by understanding, and made personal to him by conscious participation of each in all, they could serve to liberate his powers and skills instead of enslaving them; they could bring production up to the freedom and spontaneous goodness of consumption.

Where men become eloquent about the dignity of labor what else than this can they have in mind? In the history of our culture, in the record of the relations between those who command and those who obey, labor has anything but dignity: to be merely an employee is to be under necessity of taking orders from persons often morally and spiritually inferior, not infrequently inferior in knowledge and skill for the task in hand; to be merely an employee is to be under the necessity of doing what one must rather than consenting to what one understands, often indeed, of acting against one's better judgment. In sum, to be merely an employee is to be a tool with life in it. This, surely, is not what those preach, who preach the dignity of labor. What do they preach, then? They preach that which actual labor becomes when it ceases to be servile and achieves liberty; they preach its transposition from the mood and purpose of production to the mood and purpose of consumption; they preach the equation of workingman, the producer, with gentleman the consumer; they preach the release of labor into leisure. True, vengeful Calvinism at one time aspired to bring dignity to labor by degrading leisure. You remember the rhyme in the New England Primer:

> When Adam delved and Eve span
> Who was then the gentleman:
>
> When Adam delved and Eve span
> The devil was the gentleman.

This of course, does not refer to Eden, where Adam was the gentleman. It refers to the world after the Fall, when the curse of God already lay upon Adam and Eve and they had to work for a living. The rhyme was devised when merchants, artisans, farmers, and other craftsmen had become rebellious of their subjection to gentlemen born, but felt that labor was a divine curse, inveterate and inescapable. They undertook, therefore, to assert its dignity by degrading leisure, by identifying the gentleman with the devil. It is never *the workingman of leisure*. It is always *the gentleman of leisure*. We distinguish *gentleman* by the beauty and fitness of his clothes, the grace of his speech, the refinement of his manners, the dignity of his carriage, and

237

above all that by the fact that he need not work for his living but may live his life as he freely chooses.

V

The democratic faith is that every human being born is born to live as a gentleman of leisure. And the multitudes of us who are prevented from doing so, because we must work for our living, never our whole life long cease to aspire toward this liberty of the consumer. Every organization we freely form is consciously or unconsciously formed to facilitate this transposition of labor into leisure, every political party, every religious sect, every military structure, every fraternity, every trade-union. Especially every trade-union, which vindicates the dignity of labor by reducing it to the lowest possible minimum, while increasing its wages to the maximum, and by seeking for its members the participant powers of citizens in the industry. If they fail and, on the record, they do fail, it is because they remain producer-minded; because in the last analysis they are organizations concerned with earning and not with spending. Take care of the earnings, they hold, and the spendings will take care of themselves. But bitter experience has taught us that the spendings do not take care of themselves. Bitter experience has taught us that the natural primacy of the consumer is not enough, that if it is to express and sustain the liberties intrinsic to it, also the consumer function in the national economy must be organized.

Now such an organization was initiated by twenty-eight weavers of Rochdale, England, in 1844. In the one hundred years of its growth and spread, it has become a movement conscious of its basic faith, its principles, its method, its purpose. It starts today with the postulate that no man is free who does what he does merely in order to earn a living;

that free men do what they do not because they must but because they consent to, in living their lives. It is when men who work with their hands exert themselves thus—as artists, sportsmen, scientists, members of the *liberal* profession are supposed to—that dignity accrues to labor. For it is when men work thus that production is exalted into consumption, that earning one's living is ennobled into living one's life, that the liberties and delights of night life suffuse the activities of the working day. As there need not be a moral and aesthetic abyss between eating to live and living to eat, so there need not be any antithesis between earning a living and living a life.

But there is such an antithesis, and the theory and practice of consumer co-operation intend its reconciliation. They intend its reconciliation by restoring, through their methods of ownership, distribution, production, and employment, the primacy of the consumer to the first place, which it holds in nature, also in the artificial economy of industry. They are undertaking the consumerization of the economic enterprises of the national being. The need for this is being realized in other quarters, too. As the late Mr. Hopkins wrote (*American Magazine*, October, 1944), "The economic future of the nation and sustained prosperity lie in expanding consumption and raising the standard of living of the masses." And just the other day the new president of United Automobile Workers found it necessary to urge upon the members of his union the imperative of organizing as consumers. Only, on the record, these, and others beside, do not know how to achieve these ends. The consumer co-operatives do. They have behind them now one hundred years of experience of the business cycle in expanding economies and in contracting ones. Where they have been permitted to operate freely, on equal terms with their competitors, as in Sweden, they have come out each time stronger, more effective, and more liberal and liberating. They start with the consumer interest as not alone the end but also the means of organization.

It is this starting point which makes the first and last difference between them and the current masters of the industrial economy everywhere in the world. The latter, whether among managements or men, are not concerned with consumption as an end. Basically, consumption is for them a means desirable, perhaps necessary, to the continuity of production, just as the feeds which dairy farmers supply their cows are means desirable and perhaps necessary to the continuous secretion of milk. Could Holsteins and Herefords think about their own nature and destiny, would these purely artificial man-made breeds, of which the Elsie of the advertisements is the ultimate perfection, think of themselves as consumers? They might. But be assured that nothing which they are permitted to consume, nor the palatial dairies in which it is fed to them, nor the care they receive so much greater than the care allowed for the human multitudes, is anything more than an instrument in the processing of that which starts at one end as feed and drink and ends at the other as milk.

And so it is with our producer-minded economy: the energies of men are processed into things with no regard for the nature of men nor the destiny of the things. It is thus that things are in the saddle and ride mankind. It is in this that capitalism received its most telling indictment, and it is in this most evil of evils that Nazism and Communism immeasurably exceed capitalism. It composes with the miserable epic of human bondage. There is no completer waste, not even the wastage of war, than the production without consumption of the business cycle with its alternations of inflation and depression, and its *crises pléthoriques.* Of course, professional economists and publicity men for the National Manufacturers Association and the Bankers' Institute call it overproduction! Overproduction, bah! Our world at its best is still a world cursed with scarcity, and there has never been any overproduction of anything that men needed, anywhere on the globe. There has been only the frustration and defeat of the consumer in us by the weight and authority of the producer economy, its faith, and its works. Mankind have fallen into this economy by accident and those most advantaged by it have hypostatized the accident into an ineluctable natural law.

But there is no form of human association which cannot be dissolved into its elements and rearranged. All societies, however necessary we may believe them to be, are ultimately contingent. The same members may live in very many different relations to each other, and figure in an indefinite variety of different social patterns. We may set up an over-all pattern, capable of receiving all mankind, by basing it on the primacy of the consumer and so organizing the consumer interest as to insure the multitudes against the subjection into which they had fallen because their existence is cursed with the need to work in order to live. In so far as liberation is possible, the organization of the consumer is the liberation from that curse. Local examples of this pattern of freedom may be studied wherever consumer societies have established themselves; the world-wide gradient for it is already at hand in the form of the International Cooperative Alliance. These, local or world-wide, are *de facto* voluntary associations resting on the private initiative and free enterprise of each and every one of the associates, who come together and stay together on equal terms. They are the group insurance of the individual liberty of all of their members. They give this liberty a real import now, and for the future, since they enable men to retain and to build up their power over themselves. And power over ourselves is equivalent to power over consumption. It is what we have by nature from birth as consumers; it is what we win as producers when we work as an artist works or a football hero plays, as a bird sings or a dog barks at the moon or a boy kisses his girl. We then labor as free men; the labor has become consummatory, the workingman a gentleman.

As things stand, power over production is not power over one's self. It is power over the other fellow working for a wage or needing your product and unable to buy it. In the consumer mode of organization the making of goods and services is shaped to the consumption of them; the members, producing for themselves in order to consume for themselves, retain power over themselves.

Let them be farmers or machinists or men and women of any occupation which the industrial economy generates, their co-operative associations as consumers put them on what seems today the one sure way which experience has thus far shown toward an economy of freedom. In so far as liberty is organizable, consumer co-operation is the organization of liberty. In an industrial civilization it is the true region of private initiative and free enterprise for everybody, as against the lawless power of the corporation and the decree-making authority of the totalitarian police state. If freedom survives, if freedom grows, it will survive and grow through this economy.